MW01274003

Praise for "101 Ways to Have a Great Day @ Work"
by Stephanie Goddard

"A collection of powerful ideas to turn every workday into a great workday."

—Jeff Anderson, Vice President of Product Management, FranklinCovey

Dedicated to Bernie Sanders
My personal hero

List of Contents

?

Introduction

I'm no different than anyone else reading this book. I've had great days at work and terrible days at work. I've been promoted and I've worried I'd get in trouble for making a mistake. I've lain awake at night reliving a conversation where I wasn't my best or someone else wasn't. I've gossiped, called-in sick when I needed a "mental health" day and taken longer than I should have at lunch. So why am I writing this book and why should you read it?

I've spent my entire career searching for my career. I've had an awareness from a very young age that my life work should be more than just a paycheck. I watched the grown-ups around me get up day after day and put one foot in front of the other and complain most nights about their jobs and vowed I'd never spend 1/3 of my life that unhappy (especially when another 1/3 is spent asleep).

During these 25+ years (I started working at fifteen and have held a job ever since), I have read—and read and read—almost everything there is on workplace enjoyment. I specialized in college and in the workplace in human resources—the very work that focuses on making sure others enjoy their jobs and stay for the long haul with an organization. Morale, productivity, turnover, motivation, skill set development, career progression, salaries, benefits, intrinsic, extrinsic, legal vs. moral. These are words I use DAILY, not just during a crisis.

I've been trained in 13 nationally-recognized, award winning, college-accredited interpersonal and communication skills programs designed for the workplace (and continue to get certified in programs to this day). I teach these classes, and my own, every week. I've attended the lectures, the seminars, the retreats, the web conferences. In short, I've done the homework, so you don't have to.

Very few people who work full time can also devote this amount of energy to learning the advanced techniques of maneuvering through the workplace with success. If it weren't my chosen profession—in fact my calling, since I often do this studying in my free time—then I wouldn't have had the luxury of learning, trying, failing, modifying, and ultimately teaching what I have found works.

This book is set up to first address the area of personal mastery—those skills and mindsets necessary to make sure you are grounded, stress-free, and clear about who you are and who you are not. I don't think we can work effectively with others without a firm foundation under ourselves first, otherwise those skills called "people skills" can come off as contrived or manipulative.

Once you feel sure about your motivations and abilities, the book then changes focus and provides those skills and attitudes needed to work effectively with other people—in a sense, how to "play well" with others in the workplace.

My advice would be to read through the entire book, front to back and skim the sections that don't apply to your situation. Then, when time permits, focus on the sections that interest you. The book is formatted to be read in one sitting, to be taken section by section, or used as a discussion-group guide. Another option is to just crack it open to a random page each day and see how great a teacher coincidence can be.

One word of caution though: if you read an entry and say something to yourself like, "Boy, Joe sure could use this" or "I wish my boss had a copy of this," then my advice is that this is information you need to study for yourself. The tendency to identify a personal area of lack and then place this need onto someone we are having issues with is universal. It is also a great way to avoid doing the work we need to do to improve and overcome our own inability—to thoroughly examine those areas we most dislike in ourselves.

However you choose to take in this information, I wrote this with the sincere wish that you get that much closer to an enjoyable and meaningful career.

☐

Section I

Mastery Over Self in the Workplace

"Whatever you are, be a good one."
—Abraham Lincoln

Whatever You Are, Be a Good One

Jobs are more than just paychecks. They are social arenas, spiritual workshops, developmental playgrounds, group therapy, and one of the best tools for learning about ourselves. Anyone who has ever been fired from a job can tell you that this significant stressor was one of the best learning experiences of their life (albeit a painful one). Perhaps more importantly, when we are unhappy at work, we are unhappy at home too. And when we love our work, we spread that feeling around when we aren't at work.

People can't separate the two most important facets of the human existence: work and love. When one is suffering, the other suffers. You are at work eight hours a day (minimum). You are doing it for a paycheck, sure, but that won't keep you particularly productive or satisfied. What you need to keep you energized, stress-free, motivated, happy and loyal is more than just your paycheck.

Then what is the key to staying motivated day after day?

If you aren't sure if your life work is to make other's lives at least easier, then you are going to hit a wall at some point. In short, to make your work meaningful, you must see it through the eyes of working for the benefit of others. Much like volunteer work, except in this case you get paid.

For instance, I hope that what I do in my training classes makes a difference by the time my participants leave. My private goal is to ensure that they feel equipped to head back to work with a better understanding of how people tick, what ticks people off, and how to get results from themselves and others. Then, when applying these new skills back at their workplaces, this new way is modeled for customers, citizens, and even their families through example. Pipe dream? Maybe.

But it sure keeps me from hitting the snooze alarm nine times every morning.

Be a Good One Today

Have you considered what your direct impact is on co-workers, customers, or citizens? People in such positions as police officers, firefighters, or school teachers can easily connect their jobs and their impact, but what about the rest of us?

What about sewer workers or garbage collectors? Well, we gotta have clean water. What would happen if the garbage was never collected? Finance and accounting types? We all expect our paychecks in a timely and accurate way and this is probably the number one reason you work. Any copy machine sales reps out there, wondering about your purpose? I defy any of us to go one DAY, much less a week, without making a copy of something.

I often hear people say things like, "At least I'm not flippin' burgers." What's wrong with flippin' burgers? I go through a drive-thru at least once a week to feed myself or my family. I consider that important and I hope the guy on the grill that week does his job well.

Getting the point? Dig deep today and see where you contribute to the larger whole, the larger good. Don't resist this because it seems too pie-in-the-sky. It's critical that you find your calling and not just work to get paid—that you see your impact on your organization and how this carries over into impacting the city you work in, and then your state...and maybe even the world (okay—did I go overboard?).

If you don't feel lucky to have your job and get a sense of satisfaction regularly from contributing to making others' lives work better, then my advice is to start digging (hey—don't forget ditch diggers—where would we be without them?).

⯀

The Power of Habits

As mentioned in the introduction, I am an insatiable reader of self-help, and I have managed to define an entire career based on the sentence "I just read this incredible book. Let me tell you all about it!"

Interpersonal skills, motivation, self-improvement, setting and meeting goals—all of these are subject matter I just can't get enough of. However, I recently started to see a repetition in my reading. The "new" books were all saying essentially the same thing. Yet, I wasn't feeling that same "high" that I usually felt after hitting on some new knowledge that would improve my life. I was already doing what the books recommended, yet I wasn't seeing the usual results. I wasn't losing my Christmas weight. I wasn't increasing my productivity from last year. I couldn't seem to make it down to the Humane Society for my usual volunteer time. I was, well, stuck.

One of my favorite standards in self-help/business skills development is the classic, The Seven Habits of Highly Effective People. Now, I have read this book more than once, and have taught it as a workshop, maybe 50 times as of this writing. It's safe to say, I know this program inside and out.

But it wasn't until I read a book called The Power of Focus that something really important clicked for me. Even though I was teaching a class called "The Seven Habits" I never really got that this program was talking about setting habits. It wasn't called "The Seven Philosophies" or "The Seven Theories" but still, I was not clear that the message was to set (or break) habits. In reading just the first chapter of "The Power of Focus," I finally had that a-ha moment I had been seeking for so many months.

Instead of setting goals, set habits. What I mean specifically is look at your repeated actions and decide if these are getting you the results you want. When we set goals, we tend to start from a place of lack or judgment, i.e., "I need to get more organized." Well, in setting that goal, I would attempt new behaviors like setting up filing systems or trying to de-clutter my office, but this was leading to mixed results.

The problem was not so much the activity as the mindset. I saw the goal as a thing to be achieved like an item on a "to-do" list. I wanted to check off the errand and get back to the fun stuff. Consequently, I saw the goal as a burden, a chore, and my enthusiasm was revealed in this thinking. I either did what I had to do and then took a day or two off from this effort (and lost any progress) or I avoided it altogether.

Only after switching my thoughts about the goal, to one where I was creating a new habit, did I have that much-needed shift. This shift allowed for increased enthusiasm, an ease in completing a day's activities, and, finally, results.

The Power of Habits in Action

If up to 90 % of my activity by middle age will be habitual, as The Power of Focus says, then what habits do I want/need to set in place to achieve the results I want? This thinking makes a huge difference in getting results. Here are some things I have noticed that changed my thinking once I incorporated this reality:

• When I have setbacks, I don't tell myself what an undisciplined person I am or give up altogether in an attempt to seek perfection. I realize that my old habit is just still more ingrained than my new one. This will simply take more repetition of the new habit until the old is "erased."

• Once I get passed the typical 3-4 week period that establishes a habit, I will find the new habit harder to break. My "mental tug" will not be to the old behavior, but the new one.

• I created the old habit, and I can reprogram myself to follow the new one instead. For instance, has anyone just loved wine at the first taste? How about cigarettes? These "habits" took effort to become a way of life. Let's face it: these things taste awful and probably had nauseating effects at first. And yet, those who have these habits pushed passed the negative side effects in the beginning to establish a love and even a need for the behavior! Why can't anyone do the same for, say, a workout?

My suggestion to you is to start taking an account of your current habits (not your current failures or lack of progress). Then insert the new habits needed to change your results. The bad habits you have in place feel "normal" because you have done them over and over. Changing your behavior for at least three to four weeks will feel very odd, but so did the current habits during the first few weeks.

?

The Power of Habits Maintained

You may not remember your initial struggle with a habit that isn't providing current-day benefits, but it's likely the struggle existed. Even if you can swear there was no effort, the negative side-effects were likely there and ignored.

Once your new habits start providing the good benefits, they will become even more ingrained. That will be all the motivation you will need to keep the new habit and lose the old one when temptation comes around.

Our lives are created from what we do every single day. These quotes about habits continue to underscore the importance of making sure your everyday actions are ones you want to keep.

"It seems, in fact, as though the second half of a man's life is made up of nothing, but the habits he has accumulated during the first half." — Fyodor Dostoevsky

"A nail is driven out by another nail. Habit is overcome by habit." — Desiderius Erasmus

"First, we form habits, then they form us. Conquer your bad habits, or they'll eventually conquer you." —Dr. Rob Gilbert

?

How to De-Stress Right Now

1. **Eat.**

Seriously. I see many people right around lunchtime getting anxious, irritated, or sending out snappish e-mails. Once they eat, they almost seem to say, "What was that all about?" We usually don't see the connection between low blood sugar (caused by hunger) and our stress levels.

2. **If you have a door, shut it at least once a day.**

I know this can seem standoffish, but it can make a huge difference. Not only can you concentrate better, but you lessen the typical external noise associated with any office environment. Add to this another stressor that is minimized: self-consciousness. Whether you are aware of this or not, no one is exempt from feeling a little tense knowing our co-workers can hear our calls or our conversations.

If you feel that others will wonder why you are shutting your door, just communicate with them why you are shutting the door. All presumptions of People magazine reading will be dispelled!

A final note to those with doors: those without doors would really appreciate it if you would use them during loud conversations or speakerphone calls. No kidding.

3. **If you don't have a door, get creative.**

Many of us don't have a door, so #2 may feel like a kick in the shin. So what if you don't have a door? Some ideas:

•Try to build an environment around you that feels private or enclosed. Moving a desk or chair can block traffic, drop-in's and noise. Plants, bookshelves, and turning your chair so that you don't face passers-by can also work well.

• Can you wear a headset? If you aren't working directly with customers, you may be able to play soothing music on a headset to block the noise. Just make sure you can hear your phone.

• Send an e-mail, if possible, to your co-workers alerting them to special projects or high-stress times. Just letting them know that minor items requiring your attention would be best put on hold for now will help your stress level until things get back to normal. Many people aren't aware that you are under pressure.

You may feel that your frantic pace and frazzled appearance are obvious…but others may think you've just had too much caffeine! Make your workload clear, and most people will understand (and steer clear for now!).

4. **Go to bed early.**

My favorite personal de-stressor. Many people find they get a second wind about 10 p.m. and stay up reading or watching TV (late night talk shows CAN be recorded, ya know). Consequently, people are tired the next day. That alone is a huge burden to carry around for the day. Force yourself to turn off the lights once a week by 9 p.m. or 10 p.m. When you wake up (sometimes without the alarm) you will be glad that you gave yourself the time, simply by sleeping.

Try at least one of these tips this week and stress less.
?

Stress Can Be Managed, But Cured?

The term "stress" has become a badge of honor in our current world of faxes, text messages, e-mail, and back-to-back schedules. When asked how we are doing, we inevitably answer, "Oh, I'm so busy; I am so stressed out." To imagine answering: "Just feeling relaxed and enjoying today's workload," would likely mean being labeled a slacker, or at best, odd.

In developing a stress management program, we often mean exercise, eating differently, meditating, and getting enough sleep. It may be more useful to ask why these things would have to be "managed" or even mandated by a physician. Why do we have to take a class to do these things?

The answer is likely that you do not see yourself as a priority. You have not incorporated into your to-do list that you are also an important relationship that needs attention. You are a valuable tool in your life and you need to be "recharged" if you are to effectively run that life.

Once you see yourself as valuable and irreplaceable, you will naturally and effortlessly begin to maintain and exercise your body. You will not, however, follow your best friend's regimen or the latest infomercial's suggestion. You will find what works for your body, your life, and your abilities. You will like what you do to make sure your body is moved regularly and fed correctly.

While fat is stored, fitness is not. Natural principles govern our bodies, like the notion that we are not built to sit behind a PC all day and in front of a TV all night. Stress isn't something to be fixed or cured, but an indicator that you are not listening to your body and that you are not listening to yourself.

⏎

Stress Management Defined

What happens when we finally make up our minds that we are a valuable tool in our own lives? That we need the same type of preventive maintenance as our computers or our cars? What might our activities look like once the thought that we have individual and unique value and should be treated as something with value has settled in for good?

Perhaps your activities will look something like this:

When you decide to eat differently, it will not be just to lose weight and then resort back to family-sized bags of potato chips in one sitting. You will eat what you like and you will eat what makes you feel good afterward (vs. tired or nauseous). If you do not like low-fat rice cakes, find what you do like and what you know is quality fuel and eat that instead.

You will sleep because it's fun to sleep. It feels good to wake up rested. To see how much sleep you need, it is recommended that you note the time you go to sleep on a day when you don't have to be up at any particular time. Once you awaken naturally, note the time and the number of hours you slept. This is the correct amount of sleep for you.*

Take time to slow down and check in with yourself, silently and often. You may write or just close your eyes and breathe, but do not let your day get away from you through others' demands or your own unreasonable expectations without checking in with yourself.

This is ultimately stress management.

*Normal sleep times vary from six to ten hours. Experts typically state eight hours as the norm because it falls in the middle of these two extremes. You may need more. How do you know if you're sleep deprived? One clue: you don't remember your dreams.

Stress and Simplicity

One of the best stress-busters is to weed out the chaos and complexity of your work world. Here's a quote from Elaine St. James, the best-selling author of 'Simplify Your Life' and 'Simplify Your Life at Work':

"Maintaining a complicated life is a great way to avoid improving it."

Are you finding yourself at the end of a workday unsure of where the time went? You know you were busy, but you just aren't sure what you accomplished? If you answered "yes," then chances are your work life is too complicated. The complexity is creating distractions, reactive responses on your part, a dull roar constantly in the background with no time for planning, thinking, assessing.

To start minimizing the distractions and simplifying your work life, try a few of these suggestions adapted from St. James:

- Keep asking the question "Is this activity going to streamline and simplify my work flow?"
- Ask, "What is it that's most complicating my life?"
- Always estimate the time it will take to get a project done—then double it.

?

Stress and Simplicity: Part II

According to bestselling author Elaine St. James (Simplify Your Life), you can only have three priorities in life. If you work, that's one. If you have a family, that's two. What is your third thing? Working out? Church? Volunteering? You have to get rid of four, five, six (and so on) if you want to be truly excellent in this life.

You can't do everything well.

Some of my own suggestions:

1. **Get rid of clutter**.

Visually it's a stressor. We seem to take a deep breath and lower our shoulders a notch when we can survey our work area and find it in order. Not to mention most of us spend an average of almost thirty minutes a day searching for something we've misplaced in the clutter.

2. **Stop being compulsive about e-mail**.

Set certain times during the day to check e-mail. The inbox doesn't have to be empty before you can relax and focus.

3. **Life is not a race—slow it down**.

This will lower your stress levels and your error rate.

4. **Learn to say "no."**

Remember the "top three priorities" (St. James suggestion above) and only say "yes" to those when you are short on time.
⍰

Stress and Simplicity, Part III
Learning from Others Through Quotes

I am a real quote fan and hope you are too, since many things can be learned from others in our past and present. When you are faced with a difficulty, it can be an excellent use of time to search for quotes on that topic. It's as easy as entering "quotes on conflict" into a search engine. You will be surprised at the insight and application of a good quote.

Here are some quotes to motivate you to simplify your work life and lower your stress levels:

"We struggle with the complexities and avoid the simplicities."
—Norman Vincent Peale

"For fast acting relief: try slowing down."
—Lily Tomlin

"The ability to simplify means to eliminate the unnecessary so that the necessary may speak."
—Hans Hofmann, Introduction to the Bootstrap

"To simplify complications is the first essential of success."
—George Earle Buckle
☐

Water's Role in Stress Management

In any stress management regime, the emphasis on water intake is always mentioned. But why is water so important? What happens if we don't take in the standard eight-ounce glasses every day? Is it really going to do that much harm? Read on for some important facts on good ol' H2O.

1. Lack of water is the #1 trigger of daytime fatigue.

2. Seventy-five percent of Americans are chronically dehydrated.

3. Dehydration has been linked to allergies, depression, irritability, and short-term memory loss.

4. In 37 % of Americans, the thirst mechanism is so weak that it is often mistaken for hunger.

5. A mere 2 % drop in body water can trigger fuzziness, trouble with basic math, and difficulty focusing on the computer screen or on a printed page.

6. Even MILD dehydration will slow down one's metabolism and stop the elimination of toxins.

7. One glass of water will shut down midnight hunger pangs for almost 100 % of the dieters studied in a University of Washington study.

8. Preliminary research indicates that eight to ten glasses of water a day could significantly ease back and joint pain for up to 80 % of sufferers.

9. Drinking five glasses of water daily decreases the risk of colon cancer by 45 %, plus it can slash the risk of breast cancer by 79 %, and the likelihood of developing bladder cancer goes down by 50%.

Source: For more information on the importance of water intake, I highly recommend that you read 'Your Body's Many Cries for Water' by Dr. Batmanghelidj, MD.

No Random Thinking

"Show me a thoroughly satisfied man and I will show you a failure."
—Thomas Alva Edison

As an adult, you have always been in the position to determine what it is you really and truly want to be "when you grow up." No matter your current obstacles, bad choices, or credit card debt, you can take responsibility—right this minute—and start turning things around. This is true for everyone.

While some of you may be sure that you are going to spend your life in your current role, others may not be so sure. Is your current job the best way to express your abilities? Maybe you like your department, but not your current position; maybe you love your position, but not your co-workers. Whatever your current situation, it is imperative to be clear and specific on what you are doing and why and to accept that you are exactly where your thinking (the dialogue you have with yourself) got you.

Buddha said, "The mind is everything. What we think, we become." This is true in all areas of our lives, but certainly where our careers are concerned. What we are thinking regularly is given attention or mental energy. Mental energy (our thoughts) is manifested in the physical realm as action. Regular actions become habits and habits create our lives. The more focused and clear our thinking, the more focused and clear the outcome. If the desired end result is not clearly defined and specific, then it is likely we will not realize success. At best, we will get a mixed result—sometimes our plans work out; sometimes not.

Spend time this week thinking about what is happening in your career today. If you are getting inconsistent results at work—sometimes you get recognition, sometimes not; sometimes you get the promotion, sometimes not—then it's likely your thoughts are also inconsistent. When you find that you are thinking in a way that is contrary to your desires, "erase" that thought with one that more accurately represents your goal.

Affirmations Will Change Your Life

I know the word affirmation conjures up all sorts of imagery from "the new age" or pop psychology gurus, but affirmations really are more than just alternative theory. There are numerous published studies (via the New England Journal of Medicine and Duke University to name just two) indicating that affirmations work. Whether you agree with affirmation theory or not, you are always sending your subconscious mind messages or affirmations. Why not be in control of these messages?

The word affirmation is just a way of saying "affirm yourself" vs. "tear yourself down." Use another term if it helps. Input, thoughts, data, or reconfiguration will all work in its place.

Negative thinking and positive thinking are learned behaviors. We have been told by important others in our past to assess a situation as good or bad, and we continue to do so today as adults. Unfortunately, we tend to err on the side of negative assessment. We may find this more entertaining (Can you believe she wore that to the office?) or we may be buffering ourselves for fate or bad news.

The idea is that if we head off painful experiences at the pass, we will be better able to sustain the bad news when it inevitably comes. The end result is that we spend most of our lives steeped in negative thought and attract people into our lives with similar views.

Play a game with yourself today. When you realize that you are thinking negatively, look for any silver lining in the situation. Got a flat tire? Well, at least it's on a busy highway in broad daylight and not a deserted street at night. Didn't get the increase in salary you'd hoped for? You still have a paycheck. Get the idea? It's just a game—an effective game that will bring to your attention the hundreds of negative thoughts you have each day.

?

Affirmations vs. Positive Thinking

"Willpower creates nothing durable."
—Napoleon

In a nutshell, here's how affirmations work:

1. Your subconscious mind accepts all data without question. Images, words, feelings all register with the subconscious.

What this means is that if you are saying things to yourself like, "Attaboy!" then you're in good shape. If you find yourself saying things like, "You stupid jerk" than you're in for a tough ride. To test this, imagine standing on a hotel balcony—fifty stories up—and then (in your mind's eye) look down at the pool. Feel the zing in your toes? Thoughts have power!

2. Whether you currently believe what you are saying to yourself, the subconscious mind will process it as truth.

If you are trying to lose weight, simply state: "I am losing weight" or some other positive phrase. The subconscious mind deals primarily in imagery though, so watch out for negative statements like, "I don't want to be fat." To verify this for yourself, say this phrase: "I will not eat that chocolate cake." What's the first thing that popped into your head? Yep. Chocolate cake. So if you are saying, "I don't want to be fat," the image that pops into your head is likely a fat version of you. That is the picture or image that registers with the subconscious mind and you'll continue to perpetuate this outcome.

3. Affirmations are not the same thing as positive thinking.

Though there are some similarities, the technique for using affirmations is not the same as positive thinking. Positive thinking asks that you see the positive in every situation, as much as possible. While this allows for the person to focus on the upside of a situation, it may be unrealistic for every scenario (like that stranger following you in the parking lot at 4 a.m.). Instead, affirmations seek to create the outcome you would like, despite the current reality. For instance, if you find you have a chronic illness, or a troubled relationship with your boss, here are some examples of the difference between positive thinking and affirmations:

Positive Thinking (illness): This illness is allowing me to spend the time I needed all along to get myself back on track health-wise.
Affirmation (illness): I am getting healthier every day. I do things that bring me health.

Positive Thinking (relationship): This situation at work is at least teaching me that I can still be productive when someone doesn't like me.
Affirmation (relationship): I am doing things to improve the relationship with my boss. I am aware of where I have responsibility for this situation and am making progress every time we meet.
⍰

Affirmations Work

Affirmations work, but there are a few principles that must be followed:

Affirmations must be stated as if they are already true.

It is a common error to state something like, "I will be promoted soon" or "I want to be financially comfortable." Unfortunately, what this language creates is the state of wanting to be promoted, but not actually being promoted. So instead, you will always want vs. actually attain your goal.

State the affirmation as if it is already true. In the above examples, an effective affirmation would be: "I am doing things to get promoted everyday" or "I am making choices that lead to financial comfort." A good test of an affirmation is whether it feels like a lie. If it does, then you are doing it right. I know this sounds strange, but if you don't smoke and you decide to create an affirmation like "I am smoke-free" then where's the work? Where's the change? By definition, you aren't there yet, so it should be untrue (for now).

Affirmations take about one month before you even start seeing results.

This is also the time it takes to change a habit. There is something in the subconscious that just holds onto our old way of doing things. Many experts feel this 21-28 day cycle is a survival tool held over from our ancestors. The subconscious is trying to do us a favor by creating autopilot responses to free our minds for higher thinking. Instead of having to think about how to brush your teeth each and every time, you probably spend that time reflecting on the day ahead. This is one example of a habit you have established.

Whatever the reason for this delay, be aware that you will feel resistance for about one month. Resistance will look like:
• feeling silly
• being skeptical
• forgetting these suggestions and going back to your old ways

"Just do it" is my best advice for getting past this stage. Caution: Watch out for the trap of "I am becoming more skilled everyday...but not really!" or "I am being financially responsible—despite my inability to stay away from the mall" and other self-sabotaging thoughts.

The next time you find yourself thinking negatively, or in a way that doesn't best serve your goals or desires, immediately "erase" that programming with an affirmation. Remember—it doesn't matter if your conscious mind thinks it is nonsense. Your subconscious mind accepts any and all input.

Control your thoughts and control your life.
⍰

Get a New Groove

There is a convincing amount of data that confirms that our thoughts create neurological pathways or "grooves" in our brains. The more frequently we have a specific thought (or hear a thought verbalized by others), the deeper the indentation in the brain becomes. Eventually this "groove" takes the form of instinct or habit and becomes a part of who we are.

Researchers, using technology that allowed for taking a photographic image of the brain, focused on verifying this information to attempt to benefit people with mental illness. The studies took three groups of people with Obsessive-Compulsive Disorder (OCD). Here is the set-up and results of these studies:

1. The first group did nothing differently for the 21-day period.
2. The second group took medication known to repair the neurological breakdown causing OCD.
3. The third group participated in behavior therapy and focused on changing their thoughts and behaviors, repeating affirmations or helpful phrases.

A scan was taken of each participant's brain before and after the study. The findings were:

1. The first group had no visible changes to the brain.
2. The second group had positive changes and new "grooves."
3. The third group had the same positive changes as the second group.

The implications of this study certainly offer important information about taking charge of our thoughts and building a more productive and satisfying life. It takes 21-28 days to make a new groove (a new neurological pathway) in the brain.

Some suggestions to put this research to use are provided on the next page.

Getting a New Groove

No matter how high your enthusiasm may be after taking a training class or reading a new book, there will be no change unless you focus on this material for at least twenty-one days. That is the purpose of the "action plan" that you see at the end of many workshops.

You will be fighting your "old groove" for the first three weeks, so expect setbacks. Instead of seeing these setbacks as your failure to change, realize this is part of the organic process. You are in charge of making changes in your life (both positive and negative). Luck and fate may play a small role, but this research indicates that for the most part, we are in charge of our "programming" and can decide to seek out improvement or to let things stay as they are.

Pretty exciting stuff, but the real question is: What do you plan to think about for the next twenty-one days?

I'd recommend you be very precise in your thoughts. If you find yourself thinking of something you don't like or don't want or believe, immediately "erase" this programming by repeating mentally the thoughts you do want to predominate. An example:

"I am so scattered. Why do I always wait until the last minute to get things done?"

Instead of perpetuating this self-image, this person may wish to reframe this observation or trait by thinking something like:

"í like the pressure of getting things done at the last minute. I am also working on getting more organized and doing things before they are due."

Even simple thoughts like "I'm such a geek" can do damage. Instead, visualize "erasing" this groove or thought pattern by saying, "I sometimes act appropriately and sometimes mess up—just like everyone else."

Proactively creating statements to counter your subconscious messages to yourself are also useful. If you know you spend a lot of time thinking negatively about yourself, your work, or certain circumstances, erase these "tapes" and program yourself to see things the way your conscious/thinking mind wants to frame them.

Our thoughts create our behavior, not the other way around. The more you focus on your thoughts, the more positive results you will see in your interactions with others.

Jingle All the Way

The next time you get a jingle or a song in your head that you can't get rid of, use it to your advantage.

Replace the words of the song with words that affirm your goals. For instance, if "Jingle Bells" is running through your mind, replace the words with something like:

Dashing to the bank
In a four-door Mercedes Benz
O'er my office I go
Laughing all the way, Ha! Ha! Ha!

Or just….

Health, health, health,
Health, health, health
In a one horse open health, heallllllllth…

This is just one more way that you can take control of your own mind and focus it in the way you wish. It's a little like exercising—you don't realize how little strength you had until you start to use the "muscle."

Once you start to focus your brain vs. letting it run amok, you'll find yourself directing your thoughts automatically and with ease.
⍰

The Power of Negative Thinking

Remember, even if you consciously think in a positive mode, our subconscious still takes in the environment around us. With or without our approval, the subconscious hears and sees everything and takes it in as truth. To measure your positive vs. negative ratio, try this exercise:

Imagine your day from beginning to end. When you begin this mental exercise, start seeing your day from the moment your alarm goes off in the morning until the moment you reset it before going to sleep.

During your "visual trip," notice the types of input you surround yourself with. Specifically:

- What type of music are you listening to? What are the actual lyrics?
- What TV and news programs are you watching? What is the nature of the content?
- What books are you reading? How would you generally describe the contents?
- What types of people do you find in your life? What are their personal philosophies?
- What websites do you surf? What is the purpose of these websites?
- What radio programs do you listen to? What do you gain in listening to these programs?
- What magazines do you read regularly? How do these help you meet your goals?

?

Let's Talk About Talk

Notice your language starting now. Are you using words like "should," "have to," "I'd better…"? Whether you think this way or speak this way, you are sending messages to yourself (and others) about your lack of personal power. Our language is not arbitrary. Research suggests that even joking about ourselves is picked up by the subconscious as truth. Therefore, saying aloud, "I'm such a klutz!" is ultimately confirming your clumsiness as a sure thing.

Even worse than joking about our shortcomings are phrases called "Dead Enders." These phrases are a way of talking to yourself that puts off changing for the better so quickly it needs some special emphasis:

"That's just the way I am."
"I'm not a morning person."
"That's life."

Working at eliminating this type of response permanently wouldn't be the worst goal!
⍰

Let's Talk About "Me"

Now notice your "Makes Me" self-talk. "Makes me" is an example of language that is not self-responsible. It sends a message to yourself and the rest of us that you are not someone to be reckoned with. Examples include:

"Jane makes me so mad."
"Dogs make me nervous."
"He makes me uncomfortable."

Watch your language this week. It really does make a difference in productivity, credibility, and stress levels. Remember what English poet John Dryden said: "We first make our habits, then our habits make us." This is a powerful realization. Our thoughts are habits (sometimes called "scripts"), but they are habits we created.

That means we can break them, too.
☐

Never Say Never

When using the power of our thoughts, it is critical that the use of any negative language be avoided. Words like no, never, can't, won't, shouldn't, and not are simply not "heard" by the subconscious.

The reason the subconscious does not hear negatives is that it works with images only. To test this concept, say this to yourself, "I will not eat potato chips." What was the first image in your mind? I know it was a picture of you eating potato chips. That is what popped into my head too.

The same is true for all of us. "I will not go bankrupt." Immediately you see yourself destitute and homeless. That negative image is what the subconscious thinks you want to create.

Whenever you hear yourself thinking or speaking negatively (even jokingly), change that thought right then and there. Erase that programming and replace it with the image you want to achieve. "I am not poor" is replaced with "I am financially comfortable."

Even if your conscious mind cringes at such a bold-faced lie, the image that pops into your head is of a financially successful you. That image is what the subconscious attaches itself to.

Eventually, your conscious mind will catch up.
[?]

Visualize It and They Will Come

Help your goals along by giving them a little extra kick in the pants. Why not create an "inspiration board" or "vision board" and place it on your wall at work? Seeing what you want will bolster your efforts ten-fold. Here are a couple of quick guidelines:

• Use cork or something permeable to easily tack up items from magazines, websites, photos of loved ones, words that motivate you, etc.

• Instead of making the board orderly and linear, use the collage technique. If you are trying to buy a home, for example, post tons of pictures in a variety of shapes and sizes. Have fun and mix-up the subjects. Use color and symbols. The pictures may include home fronts, blueprints, gardens... whatever you want.

What should be placed on a vision board? It's as individual as each person reading this entry. What I have placed on past vision boards include:

• Hairstyles I like (and hope to have soon—come on, hair, grow already!!)
• The cover of the video I watch while working out
• My house listing with SOLD across the picture
• The mock cover of a book I'd like published
• A house I want to buy now with "Stephanie's" across the picture

You get the idea! Have fun with it. And remember—No "Shoulds" allowed (e.g. "I should put up work-out stuff 'cause I should work out").
⁇

Anxiety is Mental Clutter

Be it presentations, one-on-ones, to-do lists, family interactions…all can be handled with less stress and confusion when presented as a simple, clear mental (or written) statement: "I am attending Johnny's baseball game today. We will be on time and I will only focus on enjoying the game."

When we aren't specific in our thinking while making plans, we may find our thoughts sounding something like this: "I have to attend the staff meeting across town and make sure I drop off the request for copies before 12 p.m. I've got to be on time or the manager of the project is going to start getting ticked. I won't chat with the copy center employees and get to the meeting late like last time either. I'm going to focus on the meeting content and have lots of ideas for the group. Then when I get back to my office, I'll…"

Do yourself a favor and identify the main reasons that you may enter into situations with low doses of clarity (and therefore high doses of mental clutter). What can be done to ensure more clarity is available when needed? When you do feel anxiety, check in with yourself and see where there may be "mental clutter" that can be simplified or clarified.

One technique I use is the "twenty words or less" goal statement. If I write down everything I want to do that day and include any additional "clutter" like my stressful feelings, other people's needs, financials, etc.

I have a good two paragraphs of goals. What I do instead is type what I want to accomplish and then plug it into Microsoft Word (any word processing software will do the job) and select "Properties." Then I see the word count. Often, my count is at 100 or more words. My goal is to get it down to twenty words or less. It is amazing how much can be filtered down and streamlined with this exercise. What felt like an enormously stressful undertaking, feels light and doable.
▢

Anxiety Relief:
Think Clearly and Create Calm

*"The best way to turn anxiety into confidence is this: Be clear.
Clarity is the antidote to anxiety. If you do nothing else, be clear."*

—Marcus Buckingham and Curt Coffman, authors,
"First Break All the Rules"

This teaching complements the entry above as well as the second habit of The Seven Habits of Highly Effective People, Dr. Stephen Covey's bestseller. The second habit is "Begin with the End in Mind." This habit states that everything we do is created first in the mind. If we are unclear about our objectives or our goal, then the outcome will be inconsistent or vague, just like our thinking.

This reality is especially important for those who supervise others. If we are unclear about our expectations, then our directions are anxiety-provoking. If we give unclear messages to people (upbeat one day; grouchy the next), then we produce anxiety in others.

Decide to simplify your goals and your behavior. Be clear in your thinking. If you are conducting a meeting today, don't clutter your mind with thoughts like:

"Okay. I have to get all these things covered and then let others ask questions. If I make sure I race through this part, then maybe we'll end on time. I gotta make sure that I talk to Mary afterward about that other thing. Are there enough chairs in here? What about..."

Instead simplify, be clear. It may sound like:

"I have the agenda items I need to cover and there is enough time to gather questions. The purpose of the meeting is to convey this information and ensure everyone is clear before we end the meeting."

Imagine the difference in stress, anxiety, and confidence when you compare the first internal thought. By simply stating over and over again your one (maybe two) sentence objective instead of letting your mind race, you will naturally focus on only those things that get you closer to your goal.

⍰

Balancing Act

We all hear so much about balancing our lives, our workload, our commitments to ourselves and/or others. But what is "balance" exactly?

Is it making sure each piece of your life is equal, like a pie being sliced into sections? Is it taking 100 % and assigning a value to each section based on value? For instance, work gets 50 %, kids get 30 % and so on? Is it taking the 24 hours we each have in a day and determining what activity gets what amount of time?

I would say none of these definitions make the cut. Your definition of balance is unique, individual, and comes from paying attention to the little voices—the little tugs—you receive from your intuition or that soft voice inside your head.

When you feel guilty or frustrated or angry or exhausted or any other unpleasant emotion or physical sensation, ask yourself what this message is telling you. Are you meant to get more sleep? Is there a difficult discussion you have been avoiding? Are you staying up to watch TV, when you really want to get up early to work out? Sit with the feeling. Don't avoid it or distract yourself.

Whatever "it" is, the answer is already there. Just relax and let it in. Don't avoid it or smother it with a cocktail or a box of cookies. Each day, each hour, we can make choices—different choices than the ones we made yesterday or five minutes ago.

Instead of falling into the cycle of old patterns and moving on autopilot, shake yourself awake, so to speak. Pay attention. Do something right now that gets you closer to feeling calm, relaxed, in control, and, therefore balanced.

My definition of balance? I think it could be best described using the metaphor of a gymnast on the balance beam: Calm, relaxed, in control, focused, confident.

Adjusting to the small sways or missteps, learning from mistakes, and practice, practice, practice. Watching more accomplished gymnasts as they balance, talking to those who are more experienced on "life's balance beam," reading about the techniques, trying them out. And finally, falling(failing) and getting back up.

?

Busy Bee with No Time Free

"You can be busy—very busy—and still not be effective."
—Dr. Steven Covey

We have all had that day where we ran around the office jumping from phone calls, to e-mails, to knocks on the door, and ended the day saying, "What did I actually get done? I sure was busy, but I didn't finish anything."

Unfortunately, with faxes, e-mails, the Internet, and cell phones, we have created a world where information is immediate (and it better be). Instead of freeing us up to focus on our priorities, the priority has become, "Get the information to me and get it to me now." This makes for a fast-paced day, but not one that usually results in accomplishment and satisfaction.

The cure? Consider these two changes:

1. **Sit at your desk each morning and list what you want to accomplish in these four areas only:**

  - Mental/Intellectual (work duties usually go here)
  - Social/Emotional (relationships)
  - Physical (workouts, doctor appointments, diet)
  - Spiritual (not necessarily religious; something that gets you in touch with your introspective side, but religion is one avenue)

If you create to-do lists around these four areas, you will have a sense of getting something done instead of "Where Did the Day Go?" syndrome. Try slowing down and being proactive by implementing the list you have created for the day.

2. **Don't be compulsive about e-mails and the phone.**

It's okay to let e-mails sit for a while and let phones go to voice mail. With the exception of the customer service role, most of us can let some time pass before answering an e-mail or always picking up the phone. Many of us get compulsive about keeping our inbox free of e-mails and never missing a call. This can get so consuming that we allow ourselves to be distracted from what we are doing just for the sake of responding quickly. While this is an admirable trait, it is not the only trait worth developing.

Try focusing on one thing, then turn your attention to the requests made by others.

Managing Projects/Managing Your Life

Whether you manage processes or work on projects, at work or at home, these tips will help you organize for a better outcome:

1. Begin with the end in mind.

Visualization, and talking to others about that vision, is key. During this phase, spend lots of time (experts recommend most of the time be spent here) mapping out possibilities, talking with those impacted, creating pros and cons lists, brainstorming in meetings. You should feel that nothing has been overlooked (though the reality is, it surely has). Ask "Why?" until every answer has been given to that question.

In your home life, or in career planning, this same step can be used to plan your future. Visualize, write it down, talk to others, read, research. The more effort taken here, the better the outcome—guaranteed.

2. Fail to plan and plan to fail.

Either you love or hate this part (put me down for "hate"). Unfortunately, the reality is that your grandmother was right: If you don't have time to do it right the first time, you don't have time to do it over. Experts indicate that for every minute planning you save three minutes in implementation. In the training world, the rule of thumb is that planning and preparation is 8:1—eight hours of prep for every one hour of a workshop. In my house, we have another rule of thumb: estimate the time needed for a weekend project, and triple the estimate. Never fails!

3. On your mark, get set, go!

This is the part we all look forward to: get the new project going, start that flower garden, enroll for our first college class. The enthusiasm is a given at this point. The problem is that enthusiasm will definitely lessen as the project goes on. To counteract this phenomenon, try to see every stage as a new beginning.

Adult learning research indicates that adults like beginnings and endings, but not the middle. So trick yourself: make everything a small step/launch/new phase within the middle of a bigger project. The enthusiasm will return, and you'll be done before you know it.

4. Close the door.

This last step has two parts: One—a project should end. The term "close the door" means that you should announce the end of the project and deliver its outcomes. If you are working on processes, day-to-day implementation, then keep it going. But if you are still pulling people off the phone for meetings for an "ongoing" project, then something's wrong. Secondly—assess the outcome and the process that got you there. "What worked, what didn't?" is enough to improve your results the next time.

Organizing and Time Management

"Nothing is so fatiguing as the eternal hanging-on to an uncompleted task."—William James

Tips for time management and organization:

1. Focus on starting tasks rather than finishing them. The greatest challenge is taking the first step and getting started. It feels good to finally get moving toward a project you've been dreading. See each step as starting something new (not working toward finishing).

2. Everyday something unexpected is going to happen. Count on it. Schedule "Oops!" time.

3. Think on paper, not in your head. Writing things down minimizes confusion and stress. Write down goals, to-do lists, and even problems. Why keep all this in your head? What an effort!

4. Get a spiral notebook, date it, and keep all your notes in that book. Quit writing on loose papers that tend to get lost and shuffled endlessly.

5. When you find your scheduled "Oops!" time wasn't needed (#2), use the downtime to clear out your files. I have assumed desks with files dating back eight to ten years! Surely, these pieces of ancient paper weren't being kept for regular review. We just stop seeing the clutter after a while.

6. More on throwing away. Ask yourself, "What is the worst thing that could happen if I throw this away?" Most of the time, you can live with your answer. Most of the time, if it really was important, you can get a replacement.

7. If throwing papers away really makes you nervous, create a drawer or file to store your stuff for 90 days. If you have not used it within ninety days, you can safely throw those "keepers" away.

"What's man's best friend (besides the dog)? The wastebasket!" —
Business Week

Pride and Prejudice

"To be objective, we must first admit we are subjective."

We all see the world differently. Every one of us has unique experiences ranging from what part of the country we were raised to what books we've read over our lives. This creates a subjective and personalized method when we process information. When someone says they are completely objective, it is likely not so. At first glance, this must seem like horrible news. You may even be saying to yourself, "I know there are others in my workplace that this applies to, but she's not talking to me." Oh, yes, I am!

If you don't admit or realize that you, like everyone else, have bias, then this very bias will be incorporated into your decision-making. By not acknowledging the bias exists, it clouds your ability to assess the situation accurately. This is the harm in not seeing that we all carry bias.
⍰

Pride Keeps Prejudice Company

Another piece of wisdom that ties prejudice to pride: "When we argue, we are fighting for our weaknesses." It took me a long time to understand what this quote was saying. When we are not willing to be open to another's point of view—when we are sure we are right—we are actually fighting to keep our limitations in place. If you find yourself right this minute thinking, "I am not the person she is talking to in this entry," you are fighting to keep your prejudices.

When we become defensive after receiving feedback or argue with someone over our opinions on a matter, we are fighting to not have our minds changed. We are fighting to keep our current mindset in place. As you can probably figure out, this will ultimately make you obsolete. "Fight for your weaknesses, and when you win the battle, you get to keep them" is another way to look at it.

Today I ask that you open up to this possibility. What does becoming aware of our biases look like? How do we know when we are "there"?

The answer? When we can see that everyone has both shortcomings and strengths. Everyone (including ourselves) makes mistakes and creates successes. Knowing that we all want to be able to pay our bills easily, enjoy leisure time, and create something meaningful at work—no matter our physical form or current circumstances—is the goal.

?

Pride and Prejudice Purified

Keep this idea in mind for the rest of the day:

Each time you interact with someone, mentally frame the interaction with the assumption you don't have all the information about this person or this circumstance. Ask questions. Listen. When you find that you are drawing conclusions, search for proof of the opposite (called "contrary evidence").

For instance, if you are drawing the conclusion that this person is not a team player, ask them for an example of when they showed exceptional teamwork.

Another example: Is there someone you just can't stand in your department? Look for those things you like, admire, have in common. Try to find any common ground.

All you have to lose is your bias!

Embarrassment at Work

If you can truly say that you have never been embarrassed, hurt, criticized, or made a mistake in the workplace, then how can you be a resource to teach or assist others when they experience these situations?

Without experiencing professional anxiety, doubt, stress, rejection, and other uncomfortable (or downright painful) moments personally, then by definition you would be unable to give accurate, useful, and clear direction to others when they experience similar issues. You have no idea what they are going through; therefore, you cannot act as a resource for providing insight out of these dilemmas.

If you've never been on a bike, how can you teach someone else? Ironically, the one thing we have in common as co-workers (and as humans) are our imperfections. And yet, we spend endless energy keeping these painful memories hidden from each other. The very thing that could teach another or help someone through a difficult time (i.e., understanding exactly what they are going through and advising them on how you got through the same situation) is something we rarely share.
⁇

Errors Are Great Teachers

Appearing perfect, strong, and all-knowing doesn't serve your co-workers nearly as well as showing them that you too have made mistakes and have worked through them. In fact, I would suggest that withholding your "trials and tribulations" from others who are in need of counsel is very close to arrogance.

You may get to feel superior momentarily, but in the end, you have not acted from a superior place. You have robbed someone of the information they need to learn, grow, and perhaps pass on the same wisdom when someone comes to them with a similar problem.

Even in the worst-case scenario, you will provide comfort to the other by showing that you, too, have made mistakes and that they are not alone.
⍰

To Err is Human

By being willing to demonstrate through your words and actions that talking about, and learning from, mistakes is a necessary part of long-term career success, you allow others to share their experiences too. It takes strength to admit that you are not perfect. It takes kindness to share your humanness with another who is in dire need of direction during a painful time. And finally, it takes knowledge to provide the information the person needs to repair or improve when the co-worker has "made a wrong turn."

Show others that it is okay to be human, make mistakes, and learn from them. Pretending to be perfect never taught anyone anything, except to close off from others and hide who they really are. I doubt we will find the latter behavior under the heading of "great leadership."

Look for ways to help others who are struggling today. When someone comes to you with a problem, share your own similar experience and how you overcame it. Use your painful memories as a way to help someone out of a situation that is causing them pain today.
?

Dealing with Failure

"A life spent making mistakes is not only more honorable
but more useful than a life spent doing nothing."
—George Bernard Shaw

There are few of us out there that are at peace when faced with a failure. Failure is scary, embarrassing, sometimes expensive, and can make "getting back up" more difficult with each additional failed attempt. Hey! Feeling motivated and downright perky? Well, let's see if I can turn this segment around a little and put a different spin on failure.

You have probably seen statements on failure that sound something like this:

• You never make the shots you don't take.
• Thomas Edison created 99 different versions of the light bulb before he made one that worked.
• The Chinese character for "failure" also means "opportunity."

But this knowledge all sounds a little "pie in the sky" when you are the one who has failed. Before I offer some constructive tools for dealing with failure, I'd like to emphasize that "failure" is self-defined. What may appear to be a failure to everyone you know,* may only mean to you that you need to refine the process, practice more, learn from your mistakes, etc.

Conversely, what may seem like no big deal to others may seem devastating to you. Regardless, if you identify a failure on your part, there are few things you can do, except "try, try again" as they say. But how do you get the energy or the nerve to try again?

Mourn the failure.
It's rarely effective to try to fool yourself that you didn't goof. When we deny a problem, it comes to life; when we acknowledge it, it dies. By admitting you made a mistake, screwed-up, fell on your face, that it's not someone else's fault, only then can the process of getting over it begin.

Anger, crying, self-flagellation, brooding...whatever your version of processing a negative emotion is, will allow you to mourn your disappointment in yourself. NOTE: if you process negative emotion by eating for comfort, drinking, or taking it out on others...that's not processing emotion, but transferring it/avoiding it. Do the work! Remember this famous saying: "The only way out is through."

Then what?

Dissect the cause.
Now that you have mentally and emotionally processed the pain of failing, look at what the cause of the failure may have been and how to avoid it in the future. After all, learning from your mistake is just about the only silver lining.

Dealing with Failure:
Get Out of Your Head and Onto Paper

Processing negative emotion or dealing with something like a failure is easy to say (or write) but how exactly is it done? Are we supposed to scream into a pillow? Go to a therapist? Develop a thicker skin? I have found one technique in particular helps me deal with the hard times in life. I have used this technique off and on for many years. The more I do it, the more at ease I am. Try it and see if you don't find it a little easier to pick yourself back up the next time you fail.

Journal.
Journaling is a great way to get the "monster" out of your head and onto something more manageable—paper. Journaling is not the same as keeping a diary. Journaling's purpose: When we keep our thoughts in our head, they become larger, more abstract, more intense. By putting the thoughts on paper, you can read back your notes and see that things aren't quite as bad as you thought (though they will still be bad, as this is a failure, not a success!).

To journal, just take your thoughts and write them all down. Don't edit yourself, worry about spelling or punctuation, or that another will see your entry. A journaling session may read like: "Today I really blew it. I am so embarrassed and frankly I am a little worried about my job security. I wish I hadn't done it, but it's too late now. Hey, it's cold in here. Anyway, I would like to just stick my head in the sand and float away and never have to see anyone at work ever again. The phone is ringing—I'm going to ignore it..." and so on.

The rule of thumb for a proper journaling session is: write for three handwritten pages. That's an 8.5 x 11 page. Write for the front and back of one page, and the front of another. This is how long you need to really process the failure. Hand writing is also a way to slow down and reflect and use the right and left sides of the brain (creative meets logical). There is a ton of research that suggests that writing gets everything involved— facts and emotions—as opposed to when you just type it all into a computer.

You may find that you even come up with some fixes (or at least get the courage to apologize or some other seemingly impossible action). It's not the purpose of journaling, but it is often a benefit.

Now for the real fun: Take the pieces of paper, light them on fire, and flush them down the toilet. Worried about starting a fire? You can just tear them up into tiny pieces and flush them instead. The flushing of your troubles is great symbolism and ensures no one sees your thoughts.

Dealing with Failure:
Neither Fatal nor Final

For some, writing or journaling produces nothing but a groan. If you are not the writing type, there are still some ways to effectively process a mistake, a misstep, or an outright failure.

Talk to someone.

Make sure you respect and trust this individual or it may make matters worse. A trusted confidante with a good head on their shoulders is invaluable. What talking does is take the same monster out of your head just like the journaling suggestion above. Some of us are visual and would prefer to write it out (and some of us may be more private than others). Others are more verbal and also benefit from a different perspective. Either way, you will get a better handle on the failure.

Lather, rinse, repeat as needed.
Lather: mourn the failure (as in get in a lather).
Rinse: cleanse yourself mentally and emotionally by getting the failure into a manageable size (see "Get Out of Your Head").

Repeat as needed: Or more accurately—don't repeat. Promise yourself you'll learn from this mistake and not do it again. Or really try to find what the reason for this failure may have been...what lesson did you learn?

When I feel like I have failed, I read a quote I have posted near me at all times: "This too shall pass." Trite? Take time to really think about the words you have heard so many times before. The failure, the humiliation of the failure, will ultimately pass with time. You will not and cannot stay in this moment. Consider a failure from the past: doesn't it seem less important now? Maybe even funny? Or at least it got you to where you are today. Can't deny that!

If all else fails (sorry), ask yourself, "In five years, will this really matter?" Works like a charm!!

"Success is not final, failure is not fatal: it is the courage to continue that counts."
—Winston Churchill

Perfectionism

Perfectionism can be a standard to shoot for but becomes unhealthy when it is the only standard accepted. Some people take the goal of perfection too far... and there is a price to pay. True perfectionists are never satisfied. Chronic or daily attempts to achieve perfection are driven by feelings of inferiority and self-hatred. This not only impacts the person and their health, it seriously damages the morale of their co-workers. It is the leading cause of procrastination, ironically, as the tendency to procrastinate creates even more self-loathing and the cycle continues.

Perfectionism has not received enough attention in the workplace. It can be one of the most destructive traits to both the individual and to others' motivation and workplace self-esteem.

I have seen few personality characteristics as problematic as the need for perfection.

Are you a perfectionist?
- Do you find yourself becoming frustrated because you feel that you aren't as far along as others?
- Do you feel others (even loved ones) are always assessing you? From your clothing choice to your word choice...that you are regularly being scrutinized by the people in your life?
- Do you criticize yourself even when you are learning something new?
- Do you expect yourself to do everything well at all times?
- Do you find yourself taking part in activities in which you have little interest to gain approval?
- Do you find that when you do something that satisfies you, it is short-lived (for example, the next day you are back to trying to accomplish perfection?)
- Have you been told by the people around you that you focus on the problems in life and, even if everything is okay, you find something that bothers you?
- With most tasks, do you feel that there is a "right" way and a "wrong" way to do them and you are uncomfortable with alternative ways of getting them done?

If you answered "yes" to more than a couple of these, then I would start to work on your need for perfection. Perfection can be achieved... it just can't be the standard for everyday performance. I can honestly think of fewer reasons for hating your job than demanding perfection from others or having it demanded upon you on a daily basis.

It's really that simple.
⍰

Perfection Repaired

When you set perfection as the standard for all of your objectives, you are being unnecessarily harsh on yourself. You deny yourself the reality that you can only become better when you are allowed to try new things, take risks, and make mistakes. The necessity of self-acceptance becomes impossible and this lack of acceptance is used as a barometer for others' performance as well.

If you are deeply ingrained in the perfectionist mindset, then this information is probably being discounted by you. I urge you to just notice the possibility that you may be causing yourself unnecessary wear and tear by striving to achieve a standard that no one, but you, insists on. Read the following suggestions and select one to keep in mind for the following week.

- Remember that you have a distinct and unique contribution. Stop comparing yourself to others.
- Develop your own style and preferences instead of following another person's way.
- Stop analyzing every interaction/conversation you have with important others.
- Accept the fact that sometimes you will make poor decisions and that you will learn from them.
- Remember: perfection is not possible for humans!
▯

Feeling Inferior...It's Your Choice

"No one can make you feel inferior without your consent."
—Eleanor Roosevelt

No doubt you have seen this famous quote before, but I'd like to explore this further from the perspective of WHY we give that consent to feel inferior. There are a couple of generally accepted rules-of-thumb on why we get our buttons pushed—although these reasons may, well, push your buttons. The first reason is:

Consider the source.
The person who has criticized you matters to you. You respect them or like them or feel they have some kind of influence over your life and their comments are taken seriously. If this were not the case, you would not take the words to heart. Here's an example:

If my spouse said, "Those are funny-looking earrings," I would probably feel hurt. If the neighbor's two-year-old child came over and said, "Those are funny-looking earrings," I would weigh the comment and consider the source:

a. This is a little kid I hardly know and have no significant relationship with.
b. He doesn't have a strong command of the English language yet, so he may have meant "amusing" or "fun" instead of "funny."
c. Generally, though there may be some exceptions to the rule here, I don't find that two-year-old children have exquisite taste in jewelry.

Therefore, the truth of whether my earrings are actually funny-looking or fantastic is not the point. The point is the source of the comment. I give my consent to feel badly, inferior, angry, or some other unpleasant sensation based on the source of the comment rather than the reality of the comment.

Feeling Inferior, Part II

Another reason you may allow yourself to feel inferior is: You feel the comment is true.

On some level, you feel the comment is true. Or at least you can see why the other person feels the comment is true. It may look like this:

If someone called me a bad mother, I would get my buttons pushed, to be sure. I don't think there is a mother alive who wouldn't. But I think I am a pretty good mother, and certainly not a bad mother, so how does this theory fit?

Well, truth be told, I have had doubts about my mothering on occasion. I would also add that it would concern me if a mother didn't question her mothering skills from time to time as this would indicate to me that the mother is not taking her role as seriously as she might. Similarly, we evaluate our actions as employees on a regular basis and make adjustments to ensure long-term success, right? In fact, most of us get a review of these actions annually. Since this doesn't happen in our personal relationships, the onus is often on ourselves to self-critique and make adjustments as needed (and as you can see, I can rationalize the heck out of my mothering, if need be!)

While I have had a doubt or two (okay—several) I do think I am a good mother in the end. But if someone said to me that they did not think so, I would choose to be upset (whether I am aware of choosing this consciously or not). I would defend myself and attempt to prove that this isn't true—but the only reason I react negatively is because I'm a little worried, deep, deep down, that they are correct.

Now if someone said, "Your hair color is not ideal" I would not react in a negative way. Okay, this isn't as critical as my mothering skills—but it is a judgment that can have some sting, i.e., a person's appearance. I use this example because I have tried just about every hair color there is, and I know that my current hair color is my ideal hair color. I just chalk up this comment to personal opinion, or even poor taste, and dismiss the comment without a thought. It's just not true for me. I have no doubts about this.

The surer you are about something, the less likely you will feel the need to defend it. You don't feel attacked, so there is no need to defend. Consider the two above explanations for feeling inferior as you go throughout the next week. Where are you getting your buttons pushed? Why is feedback so hard to hear? Where do you need to make changes, and are not, because it's too hard or not fun?

Tough questions. But just creating a little self-awareness this week may help you unearth some areas that do need improvement and that are in your control.

Nothin' inferior about trying to improve yourself!
⏷

Take This Job and Love It?

Having a job or a career has its share of stress and bad days. Having a job also has its share of perks. It can be helpful in times of stress or uncertainty to focus on the perks.

Some of these perks for those of us working for an organization are easily forgotten. We tend to glamorize the life of the business owner or consultant, but the reality is that these "dream jobs" are filled with daily tedium and headaches. To give you a flavor of what is great about working for someone else, take a look at this list and start appreciating your employer more.

A regular paycheck. Just ask any consultant, sales rep, or business owner how precious this feature can be!

Benefits. Some studies show that over 60 % of U.S. citizens do not have "normal" benefit coverage (i.e., more than emergency coverage).

Socialization. Much of the research out there, states that this is one of the main reasons people stay in their job. We make lifelong friends at work.

Training. If you took a typical communication skills workshop in a public forum such as a hotel or through a management seminar company, you would pay an average of about $1200 for a three-day workshop. Many organizations provide tons of internal training opportunities. Don't miss out on developing your skills and your communication techniques for free.

Tuition Reimbursement. 'Nuff said.

Employee Assistance Programs. Help with personal/emotional issues, financial, and legal counseling. First to fifth visits are usually free (that's about $300–$500!).
?

The Disease to Please

Are you suffering from "The Disease to Please"? This popular phrase has been a bestselling book title and is heard often during daytime talk shows. But why would you need to ensure everyone around you is happy? The Disease to Please is likely coming from these motivations:

You equate worry with kindness or being nice. Worry is not an expression of friendship, loyalty, good parenting, or work ethic. It is an expression of anxiety, fear, or mistrust. Trust that others will work out their problems, just like you work out your own. Telling someone you are worried about them confirms that they are not capable of handling their own lives in your opinion.

You only identify with being a helping hand. Adding up the parents in our world, the helping professions like police, firefighters, teachers, and nurses, and you've got a lot of people who view themselves as helpers. The problem arises when you can't see yourself as anything but a helper. While this role is noble and meaningful, it is not your only function. You don't have to fix or help everyone, every time. This week, practice just noticing this tendency and then move to just sitting and observing others.

Do your best to break the habit of fixing other's problems and "over helping." You will likely start to notice less stress, more free time, and more equal relationships.
⍰

Are You Trying to Fix People?

As mentioned in the previous entry, one of the main stressors in our lives is "the disease to please." This is a condition where we try to fix other people's problems, make them feel better, let them use us as a free therapist and generally consider their needs over our own. This "disease" is in our control and can be stopped. It can be stopped politely and without damaging important relationships. In fact, it really MUST be stopped. It is probably one of the biggest time consumers and is a major obstacle to enjoying our work and our lives.

Below are two major reasons we tend to experience the "Disease to Please." Our desire to fix people or make them better is usually the motivation behind these behaviors. Provided are some suggestions for getting rid of this learned personality trait:

1. **Remember that we teach people how to treat us.*** You are 100 % responsible for being the office therapist or the "family fixer" when others are unhappy. As long as you continue to accept this role, others will take you up on it! Simply turn the tables and ask what the person has tried already to fix their own problem and don't let yourself fall into the familiar habit of offering advice or offering to take on the problem. The people in your life will subtly start to understand that you are no longer a source for "dumping" their emotional baggage.

2. **Stop feeling responsible for taking away any pain you encounter.** If you believe it is your job to lift pain from everyone who steps into your world, you will quickly feel overwhelmed and depleted of energy. Others must make their own choices to remove themselves from situations that are causing them to struggle. And remember to avoid expressing your worry or concern. Communicate your confidence in their ability to solve their problem. Telling someone you are worried about them communicates that you think they are not capable of handling

their situation. Worry is an expression of anxiety. Trust that others will work out their problems, just like you work out yours.

*Reference: Dr. Phil McGraw, Self Matters.⏹

Working on the Disease to Please

If trying to please others—to the exclusion of pleasing yourself—is a recurring theme for you, you may be feeling like you don't even know what your career goals are, much less making the daily effort to strive toward them. To facilitate removing this common obstacle, here are some insights to really focus on during this week. Place these quotes in locations where you will see them often. Review the ones you like best upon awakening and before going to sleep for one week:

"Naturalness is the easiest thing in the world to acquire, if you will forget yourself—forget about the impression you are trying to make."
—Dale Carnegie

"The person who seeks all their applause from outside has their happiness in another's keeping."
—Claudius Claudianus

"He who trims himself to suit everyone will soon whittle himself away."
—Raymond Hull

"Just trust yourself, then you will know how to live."
—Goethe

"People who want the most approval get the least, and people who need approval the least, get the most."
—Wayne Dyer

"Keep away from those who try to belittle your ambitions. Small people always do that, but the really great make you believe that you too can become great."
—Mark Twain
⏴

Section II
Mastery in Working with Others

"The most important single ingredient in the formula for success is the knack of getting along with people."
—Theodore Roosevelt

[?]

Do You Really Mean It?

One book I would recommend for anyone serious about making a difference in their career would be "Leadership and Self-Deception" by the Arbinger Institute. It's very light reading (despite the daunting name of the author). I'd like to share a concept from this work and then expand on it so that you can immediately incorporate the information into your work today:

When you are going out of your way to do things for a co-worker so he'll know you are interested in him—active listening, managing by walking around, asking about family, or using any other learned skill in order to be more effective—ask yourself this question: What are you most interested in—him or his opinion of you?

We can tell how other people feel about us, and it's to that we respond. Revealed through voice, gaze, posture, and many other signals, we can almost smell how others are feeling toward us. We can always tell when we're being coped with, manipulated, or outsmarted. We can almost feel the judgment concealed beneath veneers of niceness; or a desire to get something from us with little regard for our wants or needs. What others know and respond to is: how a person is regarding us when using "people skills."

Consider how you sincerely feel about another before using the techniques in this section of the book or skills you may be learning in your workplace training programs. Do you like this person, care about them and their future, or are you "techniquing" them to make the conversation easier for you?

Ultimately, the truth will be felt, so check out your own motivations first, then add in the techniques of communicating effectively. Using a technique is not manipulation when done in the spirit of developing a better relationship. It's only manipulation when you are using a technique to get what you want from someone, with little or no regard for the impact on them.

The Mirror Exercise

There is an old saying that points out, "We dislike most in others, what we dislike most in ourselves."

With that in mind, to remove excess negativity, resentment, judgment, or tension in a relationship, use the mirror exercise. The next time you feel angry, frustrated, or judgmental of another, flip it. In other words, ask yourself where you behave like the other person (or worry that you may lapse into that behavior and so spend lots of energy trying hard to not be "that way"). Instead of looking at them and labeling, look at yourself and make a mental shift.

For instance, let's say you are very conscientious about being on time. You wake up earlier than you'd like; you speed sometimes to make it there on time; you get upset with slow traffic; you start the morning frantic and frustrated with your family… all to make it there at the stroke of your start time. Now, let's also say that you have a co-worker who consistently "slides in" at least 5 minutes late on a regular basis.

Chances are great that you highly resent this behavior. After all, you are really making timeliness a priority and this person clearly doesn't care, right?

What's likely happening is that you are realizing that you too have an issue with punctuality. Otherwise, you would find yourself easily getting to places in plenty of time. That this other person is seemingly not going through the pains that you are to be on time angers you. This is because you feel you are giving up a great deal in terms of peace of mind and lowered stress levels to honor your priority of punctuality.

Instead of resenting the latecomer, try instead to see that you are capable of being late. We are all sometimes late! Realize that you are transferring your own self-judgment onto the other person ('cause that's easier and more fun) and continue on to the next page for releasing this judgment. ▨

Mirror, Mirror on the Wall

Here are some areas where the "mirror concept" described in the above entry might present itself:

• Judging someone who is overweight when you are dieting
• Judging someone's grammar mistake
• Being angry at someone who cancels your plans (though you have canceled on someone in your past—or would have liked to, but went even though you didn't really want to)
• Resenting a co-worker for going out to lunch (while you are grabbing a bite at your desk so you can keep working through your impossible to-do list)
• Gossiping to co-workers about how "persnickety" your colleague with the neat-as-a-pin workspace is about keeping things well maintained (and you are lucky to find your desk!)

The list could go on and on. Find your "hot buttons" and start noticing your self-talk about others. As soon as you find yourself thinking negatively about someone or labeling him or her, immediately ask yourself "Where do I do this in my life?"

⁇

Are You Buggin'?

Most of us have figured out that we spend at least as much time with our co-workers as we do with our families (eight hours work; eight hours home; eight hours asleep). Though we choose whom we live with, we usually don't choose our co-workers. If you are as lucky as some, your co-workers may become like family, but even in such an ideal situation, there will still be irritations: a poor choice of words or a snippy e-mail from time to time. If you are working with others that you already have some tension with, these events will be even more likely.

What to do? As with all the communication skills and interpersonal skills tips in this book, the focus is on what you can do, not the other party. We can't change others (though we may persuade, it's still another's decision to make a change). With that in mind, here are a few considerations for keeping the "buggin'" to a minimum:

1. Keep your voice down.

Whether on the phone or in the hallway, when another is trying to concentrate, this is an extreme annoyance. We are likely not aware of our increased volume—either due to enthusiasm about the topic or just because we talk loudly without realizing it. For those of you who are not sure if you are a loud talker...assume you are. If you are sure you're not, then you are probably already conscientious about your volume in the workplace.

2. Whispering.

While talking too loudly can be an obvious annoyance, whispering is also something that can rub people the wrong way. You are probably not talking about me, but that is what I will assume, at least initially. Shut the door or take it to the break room!

And never do this in meetings or training classes. It irritates everyone, not just the meeting leader or trainer.

3. Interrupting.

This can mean interrupting someone who is talking, but it also holds for interrupting someone in the middle of a task or a phone call. Ask permission before interrupting.

Many people also forget to ask when they call a co-worker if it's a good time. Instead they launch into a long discussion and may have to be interrupted to reschedule the conversation for a better time.
[?]

A Different Kind of Body Language

The main reason we work in a workplace is that we have to take our bodies wherever we go. Our brains may be able to work out of the spare bedroom just fine, but most organizations want to see you too. This brings up all kinds of issues like dress code, start and end times, etc. But there are some even subtler items that can cause irritation among your co-workers if not attended to.

1. Cool the perfume (or cologne).

Headaches, allergies, clouds of fragrance hanging in the air for hours…these are the side effects of too much cologne or perfume. Remember: you can't smell yourself.

After a few minutes, your fragrance doesn't register with you anymore, but it does with everyone else. (P.S. I have complimented someone's fragrance to be polite and secretly was overwhelmed by the scent. Don't assume numerous comments or compliments means your fragrance isn't too powerful. In fact, if you are getting regular comments, it is too strong by definition!)

2. Being late.

Being late for work is a different story. We know that's not okay. But for meetings, lunch, this behavior on a regular basis, is really just disguised arrogance (yeah, I said it!). It says, "My time is more valuable than yours." Now, the occasional emergency with an apology is one thing (So sorry! I got held up on a phone call.). But a habitual latecomer is sending a very disrespectful message to others.

3. Let people have a bad day.

Sometimes we have a bad day, a quiet day, a focused day…a day where we are not acting as we normally would. Instead of stopping someone and saying something like, "Wow. Seems like you're having a bad day" or "Is there anything wrong?" or "What's the matter?" just let 'em have a *different* day. These questions may seem caring, but to the receiver they are likely irritating. The message is really: "I don't like how you are acting" or "Your behavior is making me uncomfortable." Any way you slice it, the question is coming from our own discomfort with the behavior, not an attempt to soothe. We force the already-stressed party into responding forcibly with, "FNo, I'm fine. Thanks for asking," or some other polite response that probably just adds to their burden.

4. We noticed!

A loud snort to clear your sinuses, yawning aloud, burping semi-quietly? Come on! An "excuse me" will always do the trick.

Five Secret Weapons
for Increasing Your Emotional Intelligence

Secret #1—Admit your mistakes.

This doesn't mean you walk out into the corridor, stop the first person you see, and start confessing everything you've done wrong since starting with your employer. It means that many times our stress is just a bad conscience. One of the most effective ways to alleviate the burden of guilt and worry that a mistake can bring, is to just own up to it.

Your underlying concern is the fallout from being caught, right? Why not just meet it head-on and on your own terms? Have a game plan for fixing what you broke, and you will not only feel better, but you will be amazed at the impact this courageous act will have on your reputation and trustworthiness.

Secret #2—Count your blessings.

Trite and true. The reason this advice has been around so long is that it works. Human nature is to problem-solve; consequently, we tend to focus on what isn't going well, so that we can go about fixing it. Sometimes we have to force ourselves out of problem-solver mode to see the things that are going right. When you are absolutely sure that things couldn't get any worse, take out a pen and paper (or just try this silently in your head) and find ten things that are going just fine. Don't stop until you get to ten! Around #5, you will feel a shift in your thinking that will get you back on track for the day...or at least until the meeting is over!

Secret #3—Stop gossiping.

Ouch! This one is going to hurt a little, but the payoff is big. When you gossip, you are telling the person you are gossiping to that you will do the same thing to him/her when he/she is not present. It really adds up to appearing (and being) untrustworthy. Not the best trait to cultivate as a co-worker!

Gossip is mostly laziness in making small talk anyway. Instead of relying on this old standby to spark up the lunch table chat, have a few topics prepared before you get there. What if someone else starts gossiping? Don't respond judgmentally. Just acknowledge the person's concerns ("He really bugs you, huh?") and switch topics gracefully.

Secret #4—Dress for success.

This is a different take on another reliable piece of classic business information. If you are wearing things to work that make you feel fat, old, frumpy, or just uncomfortable, you are unwittingly causing yourself a bad day at work. We are directly influenced by how we feel about ourselves... including our physical appearance. You really only need five outfits. I know this flies in the face of every high school's popularity criteria, but it's true. Instead of trying to look like you have on a new set of clothes every week, just jazz up the ones that fit perfectly—and look great on you—with a scarf, earrings, different tie. You know the drill.

Secret #5—The workplace is just an adult's playground.

Keep in mind that we are all seventh-graders in our hearts. The workplace is just the schoolyard for adults. There will always be the Bully, the Nerd, and the Show-Off. Maybe more importantly, there will also be the New Kid, the Scaredy Cat, and the Valedictorian. To increase your emotional intelligence quotient, get to know these last three "kids" in your department.

The first two (New Kid, Scaredy Cat) will make you feel really great for helping out a frightened kid in a big person's body; the Valedictorian is your second chance to get some great tutoring (mentoring) from the co-worker who really seems to be climbing the career ladder (especially if your ladder seems to be propped up against the wrong wall!). So, take the new kid or the planning whiz to lunch or ask her to join your table at the next meeting. The payoff to these small acts of courage and kindness will be seen for years to come.

Communicating by Telephone:
"Are You Still There?"

One phenomenon while talking on the telephone is the necessary use of filler words. Filler words are those words such as, "Uh-huh," "Mmmm," and "Yeah" that we find ourselves using when listening to someone on the phone.

Often the stuff of great concern for those overhearing—and monitoring quality communication—this concern is likely unfounded. Filler words are a necessary evil in the world of telephone communication.

Dr. Albert Merhabian's research at UCLA taught us that when we communicate, we use three components: words, body language, and tone of voice. Following is the breakdown in percentages of how a message is communicated face-to-face.

55 % Body Language
38 % Tone of Voice
7 % Word Choice

_____

100 % of message communicated

The choice of words is surprisingly low when communicating our message. To test this, try saying the words: "Thanks for your help." Say the same words while changing your tone to:

1. angry
2. happy
3. skeptical

You'll note that the words are much less important than the tone (feel free to use this example the next time you need to counsel an employee or surly teenager on the inappropriate use of tone, by the way!)

Now say, "Thanks for your help" in a happy, grateful tone of voice, but cross your arms, scowl, and look down.

You'll see that tone and words are far outweighed by the body language (more than half).

When we are on the phone, we have no body language. Therefore, we must use filler words such as "Uh-huh," "yeah," and "mmmm." If we don't, the caller feels disconnected since they do not have the benefit of eye contact and head nods to assure them that we are indeed listening. At this point you will often hear, "Are you still there?"

Hearing this question is much worse from a customer service standpoint than any benefit gained from avoiding non-words or filler words. Instead, think of filler words as the body language we use while on the phone.

Another area of phone communication worth mentioning: be aware that some customers are not soothed by "Yes, ma'am" and a crisp, brisk tone. Research suggests that many customers find this style cold and distant. A little "yeah" or "mm hmm" here and there can appear warm and "real" to many callers.

Another tip: You have likely heard this one before, but it bears repeating. People can hear a smile on the phone. Without body language, a professional tone of voice can be mistaken for coldness or an uncaring attitude. In fact, when surveyed, many of those who do most of their work on the phone felt they were coming across as "professional" while the caller indicated they felt the employee was being rude. If you have had similar feedback in the past, try placing a mirror next to your phone. Look at yourself while you talk. You will only need to do this for a few weeks. By then your "phone smile" will be second nature.

The Handshake

The first two minutes leave an impression that lasts four years. Let's talk handshakes! Even if you think your handshake is fine, please take a minute and read these quick tips. You may be unknowingly leaving a lasting impression that is less than your best.

1. No fishy fingers.

Offering three fingers or providing a limp handshake is the worst. Your message is "I am passive; just dismiss my presence." Women do this as a form of misguided femininity. Men shake hands with women in this way to appear cordial. Speaking as a woman: it either insults me (it seems to say "You're too weak to take my real handshake") or I assume I am meeting someone very passive, very unsure of themselves. Either way, I must work past my immediate distaste. Not a great start!

2. No crunches.

When men (and sometimes) women give you the ol' grind and greet, the giver may think it appears strong and sure, but it really just comes off as aggressive. Firm is just that—and gripping 'til it hurts is not a pleasant experience.

3. Firm is fine.

Here's the way to shake everyone's hand (female/male, young/elderly): Meet at the half circle of the thumbs, firmly grip the entire palm (plus fingers) and squeeze gently. Hold for the count of one (one thousand one). Unless you already know the person well, and are happy to see them, there is no need to do the double handshake (the second hand covers both of the shaking hands).

Writing in the Workplace: Redundancies

Most of us are writers every day. We may not think of ourselves as authors, but we are definitely writers. Even within a simple e-mail, we put together words to communicate a message, and that quite literally makes us writers. Though most of us have mastered the basics (perhaps in large part to the fact that grammar basics have been "turned on their ear" in the last twenty years) there may still be some areas where we are unaware of obstacles to good written communication.

With that in mind, here are some writing tips commonly suggested in many business writing seminars for your next e-mail, proposal, cover letter or project outline:

Avoiding Redundancies

Redundant expressions create obstacles to concise, clear writing. Here is a list of common redundancies. The redundancy is in parentheses:

(advanced) planning
ask (a question)
(as to) whether
(as) yet
(at a) later (date)
(basic) fundamentals
(completely) filled
for (a period of) 10 days
my (personal) opinion
(absolutely) essential
whether (or not)
written (down)
(brief) moment

Getting the idea? Review the two sentences below and see if you can identify the redundancies:

The auditorium was filled to capacity with new freshmen.

A great many desirable benefits will come from collaboration and joint cooperation.

More words almost never mean more clarity; quite the opposite. The fewer words used to explain a concept, the more likely it will be read and understood.

?

Writing in the Workplace:
Inform or Insult?

Another common tendency that will interfere with effective written communication is "insults." I put this word in quotes because the insults are not intentional, but insult all the same. Some examples:

Obviously: "Obviously, the thing to do is…"
Patient: "We have been very patient…"
Simple/Easy: "As you can see, this process is very simple."
Claim: "We have your letter in which you claim…"
Failed: "You failed to sign the enclosed…"
Should, Must, Hereby (any words that demand or judge).

Short and sweet really is the best advice!
?

Meeting Irritations

Yes, meetings are here to stay. And it is tempting to point the finger at the meeting leader, or someone other than ourselves, when a meeting is less than effective.

But just this once, read this list of "Irritating Meeting Behaviors" and note if any of these behaviors apply to you. Resist the tendency to identify others who exhibit these traits and therefore overlook your own areas of development. Try just focusing on you and what you can do differently the next time you find yourself in a meeting.

Directions: The following list are the most common ways we make meetings time-consuming and unproductive. Even when we are happy to be at the meeting, we can unknowingly detract from the meeting with these behaviors. Make a mental note of the ones you suspect might be true for you and then work to make a few changes of your meeting persona.

- Interrupting others
- Appearing disorganized
- Appearing indifferent
- Using biting humor or sarcasm
- Being too blunt
- Taking over the discussion
- Not willing to discuss new ways or new ideas
- Using too much humor; being seen as having too much fun
- Talking an issue to death
- Being perfectionistic
- Being fiercely attached to an idea or belief not held by others
- Talking too much or randomly interjecting ideas. This also goes for whispering to the person sitting next to you while someone else has the floor.
- Being overly intellectual (know-it-all syndrome)
- Not considering other's opinions
- Proposing too many possibilities
- Being overly concerned with group harmony

Meeting Irritations: Terminal Cases

Unlike the previous list of meeting behaviors that others find irritating, this list is comprised of ways we can undermine even the most necessary meetings with our co-workers. Typically, these behaviors will be evident when a meeting member has decided before the meeting has even begun that they will not be playing a productive part in the outcome. This may be due to an opposition to the topic, a dislike for one or more meeting members, or a desire to appear more knowledgeable than the other meeting participants.

- Being too serious. Not allowing for some "small talk" before a meeting begins.
- Wasting the team's time by discussing personal agendas (i.e., "...my supervisor doesn't know what's going on in the organization," or "...my department would never go for this.")
- Being unappreciative of other's contributions or ideas
- Appearing out of touch with others' experiences/workday
- Looking for flaws in others' opinions (also called playing devil's advocate)
- Stubbornly sticking to one idea (usually your own contribution!)
- Being picky about specifics early in the planning stages
- Withholding your point of view until late in the brainstorming process

The Enemy of Excellence

"Compromise is the enemy of excellence."
—Stephen R. Covey

When you compromise, you take a little bit of what you want, and a little bit of what the other person wants—and take on things neither of you want.

Think about the last time you said "yes" to something you didn't fully agree with or believe in. What are the chances that you were fully committed to the outcome? By definition, that would be a formula for mediocrity or at the very least, not excellence.

Instead, Covey suggests that we seek "the Third Alternative." The Third Alternative comes from taking your idea and my idea and coming up with a whole new idea. Neither one of us could have thought of this new idea alone; we had to have input from each other. This input sparked more ideas and solutions, until finally, we arrive at a solution we both can embrace.

The Third Alternative is not a brainstorm (though some brainstorming may take place). It's that phenomenon where someone says something you hadn't thought of yourself but that made you think of something "out of the blue," or an idea "just popped" into your head. We've all experienced this. It's the "two heads are better than one" theory in action.

The next time you go into a meeting or are trying to find a solution, experiment with the Third Alternative. Observe yourself as you move from giving up what you want or biting your tongue just to get along—and instead become energized with ideas and solutions.

Covey believes that if we are simply willing to try it, the Third Alternative can resolve every human obstacle. It's a sure bet that the Third Alternative won't work if you don't try it, so what's the harm? Go into your next meeting with the intention of developing a whole new way of approaching a situation. Add your input and encourage others to add

their "two cents." Watch the ideas and energy flow. This method sure beats the usual my-idea-is-better-than-your-idea technique where one person overwhelms the rest of the group into doing things their way.
⏹

Risk Taking and Problem Solving

"Very few people do anything creative after the age of thirty-five. The reason is that very few people do anything creative before the age of thirty-five." —Joel Hildebrand

By now, many organizations see the value in encouraging employees to think outside the box when solving problems or creating new ideas and processes. To think in new ways and to be creative in solving problems often requires taking a risk by the employee. This risk may be social, imagined, realistic, or political.

But the very act of risk-taking by the employee and ultimately the organization keeps stagnation at bay and allows companies to thrive through changing times. Naturally these actions stir up anxiety in the risk-taker. This anxiety leads to keeping quiet and going with the crowd. The end result is not sharing what may have been a terrific idea or solution.

Even a half-idea can lead to rich discussion and variations that create real and effective change. Rarely does the group remember who started the ball rolling. We make the mistake of assuming every statement that comes from our mouth should be a gold nugget of wisdom before we articulate it. This allows key opportunities for adding insight and unique experience to be tossed away as the conversation takes on its own life with our contribution left behind.
⍰

Risk Taking Insurance

While risk-taking and the ability to be creative are valuable, these traits are most effective when used with forethought. Here are some ways to avoid failure when taking a risk:

Doing a Cost/Benefit Analysis. Even just a pros/cons list can be useful.

Talking to knowledgeable others or doing some research is also recommended…BUT DON'T HIDE BEHIND THIS! Many people won't take risks if there is ANY evidence that something is not a 100 % guaranteed outcome.

Overriding others for our own agenda. Risk-taking is not the same as bullying others into doing it our way no matter the damage. "Putting your neck out there" to improve a situation is taking a risk. Being reckless is not.

Debating is not fun for everyone. Some people enjoy "bouncing" ideas off of others and find it stimulating to debate opposing views. This is not fun for everyone and can even be perceived as a confrontation or conflict. Taking risks to share our viewpoint is about overcoming the need to seem perfect or to receive approval by going along with the crowd, not verbally sparring with others.

Focus on improving a situation, not just finding fault. Many of us are born problem-solvers or have developed this skill in our work. While useful, in the extreme it can drag down everything from productivity to self-esteem. Receiving a ten-page report and only commenting on the typo on page nine is an example of someone who thinks he is taking a risk by pointing out the error but is actually just causing friction.

This is not risk-taking, but just finding fault with someone else's hard work or risk-taking efforts.
?

It Is If You Say It Is
(or The Power of the Self-Fulfilling Prophecy)

I'd like to delve a little deeper into the meaning of the phrase "self-fulfilling prophecy," and the impact it can have on your life and the lives of the people around you.

Very simply, if you believe someone you work with is smart, you will treat him that way. Likewise, if you believe they aren't that bright, they will prove you right by responding in kind to the message you are sending them. People live up to our expectations.

Let's say I have two employees working in the same capacity. I have been given a project that I wish to delegate to one of them. It requires a lot of detail and accuracy and I have decided that Employee A is detail-oriented while Employee B is not.

When bringing them together during a weekly staff meeting, I would discuss the new project and probably say something like, "Since A is our resident detail-person, I thought I'd give A this project." While this isn't directly critical of B, it does send the message that B is NOT detail-oriented. What is likely here is that B will also avoid volunteering for detailed work, and, to add insult to injury, will rarely get the opportunity to improve her detail skills (since B isn't getting any assignments with details involved!).

"Fish discover water last" and you are likely unaware of the opinions, thoughts, and decisions you have made about others—in other words, your self-fulfilling prophecies. But the SFP is hard at work all the same. This also holds true for what you think of yourself, by the way. So now what? Well, first, start shaking up some old thinking. Deliberately assess the person in front of you (and the person in the mirror) with a balanced view.

What is positive about this person?
What strengths does she have?
What does she offer the department (our family)?

What do you like about her?
Where does she need development?
What is not her best area?
Where are skills lacking?
What does she think?
Where are your views and his off? Why?

We are complicated beings and therefore capable of both of these things: a combination of strengths/gifts and areas for improvement. We are all good sometimes, bad other times. Sometimes we can be kind, sometimes we are not. You get the picture.

Yes, it is easier to lump people into "slow" and "advanced" categories and go about our day, but it is not effective. It is certainly not accurate. And, I would offer, it puts unnecessary limits on ourselves and others.
☐

The Truth About Gossip

When you gossip, you demonstrate to others that you are untrustworthy. This not only compromises your credibility as a co-worker, but undermines your workplace relationships. Why? Because you are literally telling the people you are gossiping to that you will do the very same thing when they are not present.

The solution is to be loyal to the absent. Obviously, this is harder than it sounds or more of us would have already been doing this, so here are some suggestions for kicking the gossip habit:

1. As mentioned in an earlier entry, gossip is just laziness when attempting to make small talk. Try having some fun topics ready before your next lunch with the gang.

Some ideas are:

• movie star or political happenings (public figures don't count as gossip topics!)
• a new book, TV show, or movie
• a dream you had that you want help on interpreting
• a hobby you are exploring or want to research
• a cool website or chat room

2. Gossip generally rears its ugly head at the point where the conversation could get deeper or more intimate. What this means is that either the people talking/gossiping don't know how to get closer to others; or they do not feel comfortable enough to take the relationship to a more meaningful level. My suggestions are:

• Close down the conversation with a quick look at your watch and an exclamation: "Oh, man, I forgot about a call I have to make."

• See #1 for more conversation starters.

• Practice active listening by paraphrasing everything the other person is saying (they won't notice unless you do this relentlessly). This sounds like, "So you feel she is really coming down hard on you?" vs. "She must be a pain."

• Just listen.

I Stopped Gossiping... I Think

If someone begins to gossip, and you have kicked the habit, remember it is just as judgmental to be self-righteous about your new value system as it is to gossip.

To declare "I no longer gossip and would appreciate it if you wouldn't either" amounts to judging the other person. This is what you were doing when you were gossiping anyway, so what has really changed about you? Instead when the conversation gets catty, paraphrase, and change topics. It sounds something like this:

"So that guy really bugged you in the meeting, huh? Speaking of meetings, did you attend the new product roll-out meeting last week...?"

Expect to slip up. As with all new habits, you will revert back to your old ways. My favorite metaphor for changing a habit is the process of potty training. It goes something like this:

1st. You go in your pants, and then remember after that you wanted to do something different (You realized you gossiped after hanging up from a phone call.)

2nd. You realize while you are going in your pants that you want to do something different (You realize while you are gossiping that you are doing so, and you quickly try some of the techniques provided in this book).

3rd. You realize before you go in your pants that you want to do something different. (Hurray. It's a part of who you are now.)
⸮

You Are Wrong!

The title got your attention, didn't it? And not in a good way. Aren't you feeling a little agitation? I bet you are. This is the normal response to being told we are wrong. Your intention in reading further is probably to prove to me that you are not wrong, but quite right. And you don't even know what we are talking about yet!

This attitude is why we have conflict. Conflict is caused by the desire to be right. Think about an argument you have recently had. Was it with your spouse, co-worker, the cashier at Target? It doesn't matter who it was, or what you think about them, or even what the facts were. What generated the conflict was your need to prove you were right about whatever happened.

Dr. Robert Bolten, bestselling author of 'People Skills', states, *"My research indicates that 95% of all conflict stems from the irresistible need to be right. Our conflict would diminish greatly if we gave up this mindset."*

In any situation that involves conflict (whether aggressive conflict or polite conflict), you would be better off in the long run to give up your irresistible need to be right every time. You may wish to fight to the death on some issue that is important to you—and those fights are likely the ones that define who you are and what you stand for. But when you are fighting over who took out the garbage last and whether you were actually the next one in line, you may need to see where your need to be right is getting in your way.

[?]

Being Right:
What Price Do You Really Pay?

"There is no perfection in humanity."
—Samuel Montagne

Recently I had the opportunity to speak with several employees about their views on conflict, dealing with difficult people, what to do when you are responsible for a project (but don't have the authority), and how to get things done when others aren't cooperating.

I was surprised by how many people basically said, "They are wrong and I am right and I will continue to remind them of that until they do what they need to do." These weren't the exact words, of course. These words are a summary of several twenty to thirty minute conversations, but "They are wrong and I am right," says it in a nutshell.

I was stunned that no one considered problem solving, setting up a meeting to discuss both perspectives, or asking for advice from someone with more experience. It seemed these folks were simply comfortable with being right (in their opinion) and that rightness would prevail.

But being right and being *effective* are not always aligned. Sometimes you have to push aside your reason, logic, and negative opinion of another to do a good job—be it at work or home. Being right, in my mind, is not standing stubbornly in defense of your position. Instead it is about getting what you want or need from a situation to continue interacting effectively.

Did you meet the deadline? Is everything working smoothly? Are people communicating better? Did we come in at or under budget? Is my child adjusting to school? Will we be able to retire without financial anxiety?

I guess what I am saying is RIGHT LIVING is more important than BEING RIGHT. Instead of arguing or talking about someone negatively or sending defensive e-mails, how about trying something different?

- Use your best communication skills (these are sometimes referred to as "manners")
- Work past your ego
- Stop trying to give the impression that you are perfect
- Work toward getting a good night's sleep (I know BEING RIGHT can keep one tossing and turning I've had a few of those nights myself!)
☐

Aggressive, Assertive, or Passive: Which One Are You?

When surveyed, 80 % of those asked this question stated that they were assertive. After long-term observation, it was determined that only 20 % of the population surveyed responded in a truly assertive manner (60 % ignored problems/conflict; the other 20 % lost their temper).

What is assertive behavior? How does being assertive help us with conflict in relationships? How can it help us get what we want in life?

Assertive has been described by Dr. Stephen Covey as "courage balanced with consideration." This means that you have the courage to state your needs or feelings, but you don't offend the other person (and you are willing to hear the other person's wants and needs too). In simpler terms, this could be described as having the guts to speak up. But remember to balance this with some manners.

Aggressive is being more concerned with your own needs and having little or no regard for the other person's position. "My way or the highway" is aggressive, no matter how nicely you put it.

Passive is caring more about another's needs and ignoring or minimizing your own. People-pleasing and conflict-avoidance at all costs fall into this category too.

Now that you have full definitions...which one are you?
⁇

Being Assertive:
Communication's Goal

Now that you know the mindset you need for assertive thinking (see above entry), the next few entries offer some suggestions for appearing assertive (in other words, "fake it till you make it!"). Notice your body language. As mentioned earlier, 55 % of your message is communicated through your body. What does assertive body language look like? Do you make eye contact, but avoid staring (or glaring)? Making no eye contact can be perceived as shifty, dishonest, or insecure.

What are you doing with your arms and your hands? A crossed-arm position indicates being closed-off or not open to hearing the other person. Hands in pockets, held behind back, tucked into long sleeves or in the "fig leaf" (clasped in front covering the lap area) are all passive signals. Keep hands cupped slightly at your side for an assertive response.

Keep face neutral with a slight closed-mouth smile. Don't furrow the brow or turn down the mouth (aggressive). Avoid excessive head nodding (passive).

When standing, keep legs hip width apart. Closed tightly says passive. Wide-spread (think "superhero") is aggressive.

When sitting, lean forward to indicate interest. Leaning back with arms locked behind your head is aggressive; hunched with hands in lap (or fiddling with paper clips, rubber bands, etc.) is passive.

Spend this week noticing your body language. This is time well-spent. The more you notice and control your body, the more routine appearing assertive will become for you. When you do get into an argument or have a conflict, you'll be able to focus on your thoughts, words, desires, or goals because you have already mastered 55 % of your message before you find yourself under pressure.

Being Assertive:
Communication's Goal, Part II

Now that you have focused on the body language, you are ready for some suggestions for sounding as assertive as you look in an interaction:

Notice your tone and volume.

As 93 % of our communication is nonverbal, paying attention to our tone becomes vital, especially with 38 % of your message being communicated through tone of voice and volume.

Use your "pass the butter" voice. Right this minute say aloud, "Please, pass the butter," as if you were at the dinner table with your family. This is the right tone and volume for an assertive conversation.

If someone is being aggressive with you, take the "pass the butter" voice down a notch. This will help calm the other person, but be careful: getting too quiet or talking slowly will either further anger the person (they will feel patronized) or they will assume you are passive and can be bullied.

Tone conveys the very essence of our message, making words a distant second. Focus on your tone today, not your word choice. We have spent years mastering our vocabularies and virtually no time at all monitoring our tone and volume. Imagine saying, "Pass the butter" angrily, with sadness, with glee, or with excessive volume. See? Completely different message!
⏀

Being Assertive:
Word Choice is Your Choice

Only 7 % of our communicated message involves words.

Amazing! We spend so much time thinking about what we are going to say, that we forget that 93 % of our message is coming from our body and our tone. However, words do have power. Unfortunately, we often use them to our disadvantage. We fib, we exaggerate, we manipulate, we understate. We try to win arguments instead of conveying our thoughts fully. We take positions more than we communicate our real interests or desires.

Words to avoid are a good place to start. Here are some words that get people mad almost immediately:

Never
Always

What's wrong with these two words? Well, they are absolutes. And people are absolutely, never, always a certain way. If I am arguing with you about the last person to take out the trash, I might try to win the argument by saying "You never take out the trash." We have all been on the receiving end of such an inaccurate and unfair statement. This type of absolute never lands well. If you are trying to communicate your interest of the unequal distribution of labor in your household, you will want to come at it with actual facts. This may sound something like, "The last four trash days, I took out the garbage."

Likewise, in a workplace scenario, if I am discussing my employee's late arrival I would not state (as so commonly happens), "You are never on time." At best, this will start a memory war of the last time the employee was on time (I was early three years ago and you didn't even notice) or a deflection to other late-arriving employees (Linda's always late and you aren't talking to her about her tardiness!).

Better to state the facts once again: "On Monday and Tuesday, you arrived fifteen minutes late; and on Friday you were twenty minutes late."

Watch your all-or-nothing language and find yourself in less hot water. ⍰

Senseless Confrontation

Many of the programs I teach center on the need for communication skills training as they pertain to conflict or defensiveness that can arise when someone confronts another in the workplace.

I have spent a good deal of time teaching people how to confront effectively, i.e., without creating tension in the relationship. This is accomplished by choosing our words carefully; noting our body language; paying attention to our tone of voice—in essence, by doing a "reality check" on the intention and attitude and how these show themselves in our actions—before confronting someone.

This internal check ensures that the reasons for confronting another are good reasons.

This explanation begs the question: "What is a good reason to confront someone?"

In the workplace, the answer is always: when the behavior that is in question is work related. Issues such as hairstyle or complaining about another person's messy work area when the person is producing just fine and can find documents easily, are examples of topics that are not work related that get people in trouble.

Only focusing on work-related behavior, therefore, makes the most sense and is actually a requirement for those in management. As a supervisor, part of the role is to give work-related, objective feedback on observed behaviors that need improving in order to do the job more effectively. Managers must do this regularly or risk losing their own jobs.

But what about those situations that are not work related? What about the surly computer tech servicing your PC? What about the coworker who doesn't report to you but still works with you? How do we confront these people effectively?

My answer is "You don't."

I have come to the conclusion that there is never a good reason to confront someone about his or her behavior when it is not required by your job description. To confront someone and insist they change their behavior, personality, or lifestyle is actually quite ineffective (not to mention pretty darn cocky) even if it's "for their own good." Anyone that has ever confronted someone knows this. I am willing to bet the results were terrible about 100 % of the time (okay—99.77 %—but I bet that person was ready to change anyway!).

Every single job description in the world is simply this: To manage results while simultaneously maintaining relationships.

If you are confronting someone and the reason is not job-based results, you're asking for damage to the relationship.
⁂

Senseless Confrontation Alternatives

When we confront someone on personal choices such as personality, values, politics, religion, or traditions, we automatically set up a scenario that begs that person to defend his very essence. We are seeking out nothing less than asking this person to give up those things that are most dear to him or her—just because we told him to.

No one comes to the decision to express an important idea, get a tattoo, belong to a certain club or political party, or to celebrate Kwanzaa without some emotional investment and forethought. To question and devalue this choice is to question and devalue how that person defines themselves. This is just too personal an area for another person to get involved without expressed permission—and is frankly, none of your business.

Though you may feel this person will be happier (or you feel you have the right because you are related or a friend), you are making an assumption that is just too stacked against you to really do anything but increase the tension. I guarantee you a confrontation will never lessen the tension. You may get what you want in the short run, but it will catch up with you in the long run. The solution?

Don't confront. Stop confronting. Confrontation is always senseless. Instead:

• Lead by example then wait until asked for your input.
• Discuss a book you've read that addresses the topic.
• Just bite your lip (while asking yourself why you are so adamant about changing this person).
• Stay polite and keep the topic light.

"Be not angry that you cannot make others as you wish them to be, since you cannot make yourself as you wish to be."

—Thomas a Kempis

Don't Make Me Ask

Maybe it's me, but I've never been good at breaking the ice when it comes to getting the cold shoulder. Funny how those two expressions go together!

I have experienced the cold shoulder in the past from a co-worker for reasons unknown to me. And how have I, the trainer of all-things-conflict-riddled, handled it? I simply trusted that whatever "it" was, if it was really important, would be brought to my attention. I just kept working and being polite and minding my own business. After a time, things went back to normal, and I was none the wiser.

Now the question that is begging to be asked is, "Is this a good way of going through life, dealing with co-workers and loved ones?" Well, I would say "yes" since that's my way. But let me tell you my rationale and then see if it fits for you too.

I see it this way: I can't read your mind, though I can read your body language. But if you are angry with me, or judging me, why do I have to go further out on the ledge and take the risk and actually ask for more discomfort undoubtedly at my expense? Why shouldn't the discomfort be on *your* end by having to have that difficult conversation in which you present your contention to me, and we hash it out, and hopefully resolve the difficulty or difference of opinion?

I realize that the cold shoulder is supposed to push me into taking the first step and saying, "Gosh, is something bothering you?" therefore opening the door for the upset person to relieve himself of his tension or distaste. But as the title of this section says, "Don't Make Me Ask," I gotta say I think it's unfair. To be both mad at someone and show it physically and then make them get it out of you is a double-whammy. At least meet that person halfway. After all, you're the one who is steaming. It's your pot that's boiling over, why do I have to move it off the burner?

So, what this advice is suggesting is instead of stewing, take on your issue with the person directly--and soon. I know that the longer I let something fester, the worse it becomes in my head. I think this does a lot of damage in the end. Better to just get it over with, like pulling a thorn out of your palm. As always, I ask that you look at the applications for this both at work and home. Spouse and kids can't read minds either!

"Get mad, then get over it." —Colin Powell

Understanding Angry People

Most of us have to work with citizens, customers, vendors, suppliers, etc. And unfortunately, these interactions can sometimes be tinged with anger. Aside from the normal customer service behaviors we rely on when someone displays anger, what else can be done?

The most common answer I get when I ask what someone does to deal with an angry customer they say, "Let them vent." Okay. That's good for starters. The problem with this technique is that often a customer decides that you are willing to be dumped on; that you'll take their bad day off their shoulders; that you'll put up with a great deal of negativity. Not exactly a formula for lowering stress and problem solving.

What I find helps is to understand anger, not try to understand the content of why the person is yelling. Anger is actually a secondary or learned response for two other emotions: fear or sadness. Anger has been identified by behavioral scientists through this research as an emotion that is actually a distortion of fear or sadness.

If you look at the citizen whose water is being turned off for the weekend and his anger is through the roof, what emotion do you think he is really feeling? How must it feel to be "losing it" to the degree that you no longer have water? What else is happening? Lost job? Other utilities being shut off? Will this citizen's kids be able to bathe or get a drink this weekend? Imagine the fear, the sadness. But all you get is the "puffing up" to try and counter this person's worst fear that has just become a reality: he is not going to get what he needs and it's his fault.

What about the mom who is signing up her son for soccer and missed the deadline and is throwing a fit at the front desk? Is she scared or sad? Yep. How would you like to go home and tell your kid that you messed up and everyone else is going to get to play soccer, but not him, 'cause mom blew it? Same emotions, same response.

All of this background information on anger is being presented here in the hope that you can shift your thinking when dealing with anyone who is angry or upset. Compassion will likely replace having your buttons pushed. Your tone of voice, body language, and word choice will all be reflected in this shift and the person will naturally respond.

?

Using the Law of Entrainment

Entrainment is a physics term. It is a physical law that shows "the stronger will always pull the weaker toward it."

Entrainment can be witnessed when a car tailgates a truck and the truck's acceleration force pulls the car along with no acceleration from the car (not recommended here!). The largest clock in your home will pull the smaller clocks to its beat until they all beat in sync.

How is this information useful in a business setting? When we experience strong emotions from another (i.e., anger, silent treatment, etc.) we are initially inclined to respond in kind. If I yell at you, you will be entrained to that strong energy and likely yell back (or want to). But if you keep calm, refuse to respond angrily and genuinely work toward resolution—that response is harder—and therefore the stronger force. I will then lower my emotion to match yours.

This is especially important to those of you "on the frontline." Be it a police officer or a customer service rep, you experience strong emotion on a regular basis. Those who have worked with upset customers on a regular basis already know about entrainment, even if you've never heard the term before: staying in control of your emotions (and not allowing the other person to "entrain" you) will result in you being the stronger force and therefore entraining them to your level.

Customers, co-workers, and citizens inevitably calm down and even apologize when we stay calm, polite, and helpful.
⧠

Where's Your Conflict Coming From?

"When we fight, or argue with another,
we are fighting against having our mind changed."
—Mahatma Gandhi

If you are absolutely sure of your position in a certain situation, then how would it be possible to ruffle your feathers when you are faced with the contrary opinion? If you are 100 % sure of your position, you will be able to relax and listen to someone else's perspective with confidence, even curiosity, i.e. "Why do they think this way?" or "What have their experiences been to create this opinion?" The next time you find yourself getting your buttons pushed, consider that you may not be as sure of your position as you think. Therefore, what would be the harm in getting a little more information?

The next time someone gives you constructive criticism or suggests that you might handle something differently or better, resist the urge to defend yourself or challenge the information. If you do resist or challenge, you are in effect arguing to stay where you are right now. For the most part, people give you constructive feedback to help you progress. If they didn't care, they'd let you fail. Now go back and re-read the quote at the top of this entry with this explanation in mind.

Regardless of what you may read or hear, outwardly expressing every feeling you have is not realistic, especially in the workplace. Instead, you may be better served to acknowledge to yourself how you are feeling, sit with it for a minute, and then take action or let the matter drop. If you have the luxury of being in your car, or some other private place, then let out a yell, bang on the steering wheel, or whatever you need to do. Another technique is to write a "rage letter." This letter gets out all you are thinking and feeling about a person or situation on paper, and ultimately purges you of these feelings (of course, it must be destroyed after writing it!).

To try and pretend you don't feel a certain way, or to suppress that feeling is not a long-term formula for effectively handling uncomfortable feelings. Eventually these feelings will make themselves heard...through resentment, lack of motivation, and even illness. Sometimes you just gotta feel the pain! Lean into it, don't avoid it. That's the only way to transform it.

Co-worker, Thy Name is Friend

If you have worked in an organization for any length of time (a year or more), and keep almost everything about you concealed, ask yourself why. Why would letting your co-workers get to know you make you concerned? About what? Gossip may be a factor. Are you worried about a relationship turning sour and someone having all your secrets?

This isn't about making your coworkers into free therapists. Instead, it's about recognizing that we are very much the same at the core. People want to be asked about their families, their weekends—and want to hear about yours too. This give-and-take lends itself to the most important component in any capacity: trust.

Are you confusing professionalism with isolating yourself (insulating yourself?) from others? You may be unknowingly creating a tone that says, "I don't trust you, so I won't show you who I really am." Someone who is very closed, not open to small talk or other forms of relationship building, ultimately makes me suspicious. I know that's a strong word, but that kind of behavior does make me wonder, "Why is he so secretive? Angry? Resistant to others? What's going on in his head?" I'm sure that's the exact opposite impression this person had hoped to create.

Keeping a professional distance may make sense in some situations, but in general, I would encourage you to relax and enjoy the people you work with.

> *"Better to trust everyone and be occasionally wrong,*
> *then trust no one and be occasionally right."*
> —Unknown

[?]

Friends Are Not Optional

Developing a friendship with a co-worker who has a work ethic you admire and someone who can "keep it zipped" is a must-have. No matter how great your significant other, friend, or neighbor is at solving problems or listening to your work concerns, they are not your best option.

Why? *BECAUSE THEY DON'T WORK HERE.*

You may have done a fine job of explaining the personalities, the culture, the issues, but someone who does not work where you work cannot fully take in the whole picture and provide you with the best advice possible.

When you are able to shut a coworker's door and say, "Was Mike being hard on me during that meeting, or am I being too sensitive?" that's worth its weight in gold. Getting a reality check from someone who can see things more clearly than you at the moment, or offer advice on what to do next, is key to career success and satisfaction. Naturally, this person needs to have a value system where your information will not be shared with others—otherwise you're just unintentionally gossiping!

According to a recent Gallup poll, employees who have a best friend at work are seven times more likely to be engaged in their work than those who did not have a best friend at work (those without a best friend at work were only one in twelve self-defined as being productive and happy at work).

Many nationally recognized training programs suggest finding a "coaching peer." This is essentially finding a trusted confidante within your workplace to run things past; someone who is able to give you some sound ideas when handling a tough situation, or give feedback when practicing a presentation, etc.

And hey, just being able to vent or have a laugh can relieve stress and keep you from spending needless energy stewing about a work-related concern.

For that you need a friend.
?

Balancing Pride with Humility

"Greatness is a two-faced coin—and the reverse is humility."
—Marguerite Steen

Ah, pride. Not enough, and you wouldn't be where you are today. Too much, and you will find yourself eating lunch alone!

So what's the right balance? Humility.

Humility is often misinterpreted as humiliation and the two words are worlds apart. Humility is the realization that we all have strengths and weaknesses, and that our embracing and accepting these traits is critical to success and contentment.

One technique that can be very useful in increasing your humility is taking a self-inventory. This inventory is an honest look at what you have to offer: your gifts, talents, traits, skills, education, and other assets.

The next step is to balance this information with those things that need work, could be improved, or will just never be strong in you. Resist "playing humble" and overstating your weaknesses. This mindset isn't useful for this exercise.

Once you have these things on paper, you can work with others with the inner confidence that you now know who you are (and who you aren't). If someone asks, "Are you any good at presentations?" you can say, without it sounding like bragging, "Yes. I'll be glad to handle this." If you are not good at presentations—and never will be in your current opinion—you might respond, "Presentations have never been my strong suit, but I'm pretty good at researching data. How about I handle that piece?"

This allows you to put into full use your strengths and to stop hiding your weaknesses.

Create a self-inventory starting now. This is for your eyes only (even spouses are off-limits). Resist doing this in your head. Write it out to get the full "left brain, right brain" benefits. Be honest while creating this list. Spread this exercise out over a minimum of a two-day period.

?

The Damage of Mistrust

Many nationally-recognized communication skills workshops discuss the concept of trusting others and being trustworthy as their basis or foundation. The elements of why trust is so vital to the health of an organization, work group, department or relationship is:

1. The quality of relationships is negatively affected when actions or words say, "You are not trustworthy" or "I am not trustworthy."

2. The quality of relationships (be they work or personal) is the only true measure of success in your work and personal lives.

3. The quality is measured in terms of trust and trustworthiness.

Let's break this down a little further...

Lack of trust and the impact to an organization or department/work group:

- Lack of trust lowers morale and increases turnover
- Productivity is negatively affected as employees feel their behaviors are suspect
- Problem-solving becomes unimportant or futile
- Self-initiative is viewed as a potentially self-defeating action or punishable offense
- Doing just enough to avoid disciplinary action or termination is the benchmark for performance impact to personal relationships
- Actions that create the message "I don't trust you" will create barriers between you and important others
- Important conversations or "clearing the air" are avoided
- Current issues or concerns are kept to yourself potentially resulting in heightened conflict
- The general mindset is, "Why should I give 100 % when 'my all' is questioned (i.e., not trusted)?"

Do I Have to Trust Everyone?

When is a lack of trust normal? When you meet someone new or bring on a new employee, it is natural to hold back and let that person prove a level of trustworthiness. Likewise, anything that involves personal or public safety needs a "close watch." After that, showing someone you do not trust them, or at the very least are wary, takes us back to the premise above:

The term "quality" in a relationship is measured by the level of trust in that relationship.

Suggestions for breaking through mistrust
- Doing what you say you will
- Being loyal to the absent (no gossiping)
- Showing courtesy and manners
- Apologizing when needed
- Being transparent
- Willing to continue improving oneself and relationships with others
- Honoring expectations
- Not assuming prematurely that others are incapable of the actions listed (often called "micromanaging")

Then ask yourself:
- Am I strong in these areas in my important relationships? If not, what can I start doing to get back on track?
- Is someone showing low levels of one of these and that has created a lack of trust on my part? What can I do to improve the situation?

Give it some thought. You may find that you will be improving your relationships—both in and out of work—by showing you are willing to trust others and that you are trustworthy.

?

Your External Appearance

"Expecting the world to treat you fairly because you are a good person is like expecting a bull not to attack you because you are a vegetarian."
—Dennis Wholey

Yes, this entry is emphasizing the importance of something as superficial as your external image.

In actuality, it would be irresponsible of me to suggest anything different. The reality is that we live in a society bombarded with visual images all day, every day. Some of the sources of our external, visual focus are MTV, magazines, billboards, and the Internet, all providing visual stimulation at lightning speed. The result is that we have become a society of highly-advanced visual experts. We can look at an image for approximately five seconds or less and have an accurate, lasting impression, says 'First Impression, Best Impression: The Four Minute Sell.'

The truth is that we are assessed by our outside appearance—quickly and effectively. With rare exception, if the "outsides" pass muster, then time will be taken to get to know the "insides." How we dress and how we choose to look are all part of communicating with others.

In the animal kingdom, birds fluff up their feathers to appear bigger, and rabbits freeze in natural brush to appear invisible and avoid attack. Dogs bare their teeth to indicate aggression. As human animals, we do the same thing. We wear black to appear leaner. By appearing leaner, we might be showing we are healthy, fit, and active (survival of the fittest!). We wear heels to appear taller, because taller might just mean stronger (recent reports have indicated that taller people are promoted more often than shorter ones, so this behavior may not be off the mark!). We sunbathe or "fake tan" to appear darker, because a sunny glow means health and health means strength.

We can, and do, alter our natural appearance to give the impression we want to give, so that we can get what we want from others. "Getting what we want" is just a modern way of saying survival. We must get what we want (and need) to earn the income that provides food, shelter, and clothing, i.e., the survival tools of the human species.

Add to this reality, that most workplaces have a standardized—usually non-published—dress code. Yes, most workplaces have a "uniform" (and I don't just mean for firefighters, police officers, or medical personnel). And like all uniforms, its role is to help clarify who you are (or who you are not) based solely on how you appear visually.
?

External Appearance Matters

To show how your appearance really does matter, let's look at a non-business or non-government environment we can all relate to: the doctor's office. Imagine you are waiting in the examination room to meet your new physician. Soon, she enters the room wearing a tight-fitting Mickey Mouse t-shirt with short cut-off denim shorts and a pair of flip-flops. You have to admit, no matter how open-minded you may be, you'd be fighting every impulse to say, "Who are you? You can't be the doctor!"

You might even recoil at her initial touch. What you were expecting was the standard "uniform" of the medical profession: white jacket with sensible shoes, a stethoscope, and possibly a name tag. At the very least, you expect to see green operating scrubs and an ID badge.

And that's how it is everywhere. We expect to see a certain "uniform." Customers expect a certain look from an employee and will immediately form an impression of the entire organization based on, of all things, your clothes, hair, jewelry, and other seemingly irrelevant items.

Case Study:
When I began working with Carrie, she was angered by her lack of progress up the corporate ladder even though she was clearly more skilled and worked as hard, or harder, than anyone else in her department.

Carrie arrived in my office straight from work in a polyester "stretch" pantsuit in a drab dark brown with matching foam-soled shoes. Her hair was cut very short and looked dry and brittle. She wore no makeup and carried a beat-up backpack. After reviewing her credentials and current projects, it was clear that Carrie didn't need work on her abilities or skills. What needed adjusting, in my opinion, was only her external image.

Carrie was very resistant to changing her appearance. She argued that this went against her value system and that anyone who was judging her by her appearance didn't deserve to be catered to. Ironically, after further discussion, it became clear that Carrie was unconsciously dressing and grooming herself to make this very statement to others, i.e., "Don't you dare assess me by my looks, but you better notice that my looks are harsh, dark, and no-nonsense, just like me."

For all of Carrie's resistance to this concept, Carrie was unconsciously doing the very thing she judged others for doing—dressing to send a message.

We all do this, whether we realize it or not. What's inside us can, and is, reflected on the outside in the form of our external appearance. If you are interested in having an easier time establishing your credibility and commanding attention vs. fighting disinterest, then you would be wise to ensure more than just the skills required to do your work. One of your first tasks is to make sure your appearance advertises your intention of competence and success.

⁇

A Special Section for Supervisors

Feedback:
The Dirtiest Word in the Workplace

Feedback has been hailed as the most powerful tool in the modern workplace. So why do we hate to use it and what can be done about it? After years of researching interpersonal skills and then training supervisors and managers on the fine art of giving feedback, I think I have finally figured it out, but I would appreciate your feedback!

Recently, I had the opportunity to test the necessity of feedback. During a simulation exercise, I was given a picture of a maze and detailed directions. These directions were given to me both in writing and verbally, providing information on how to move the pencil by inches, when to move upward, and other specifics. The directions were provided to ensure I made it out of the maze successfully. I was encouraged to refer to the directions throughout the exercise. I was then blindfolded and told to begin.

I failed miserably.

Why? Because getting directions, no matter how clearly created and beautifully executed, cannot replace step-by-step feedback. Just imagine if someone had been behind me watching my moves, urging me along when I was headed in the right direction, and giving me corrective information when I got off-track. I would have undoubtedly made it out of the maze. I think this is a relevant analogy for the function of feedback in today's workplace.

Those employees that do make it out of the "departmental maze" are either lucky, have had some inside information from a mentor or other knowledgeable co-worker, or have been through it enough times that they know the pattern. The result is a mixed outcome of successes and failures, leaving a supervisor scratching her head. Some of her employees are succeeding, some are not, and she can't determine what to keep doing and what to stop. It is feedback that will make the difference between the successful employee and the unsuccessful, so why is no one doing it?

Unfortunately, the reason is partly due to the fact that most employees associate the term feedback with criticism. This leads to tremendous stress for both parties and general ill feelings for several days following the session. It doesn't have to be that way. Read on for valuable tips and insights into giving effective feedback.

[?]

Feedback:
How It's Done

Following are the steps I recommend for changing the negative perception of feedback. These steps will work in any organization—be it work, family, or school.

Watch Your Language. If you are experiencing a strong negative reaction to the word feedback, don't use it. Instead of calling someone to your office to give them feedback, tell them you have some information about their latest project. Other terms might be results, tips, numbers, or impact.

Avoid "May I See You in My Office?" Syndrome. Give feedback regularly, not just when something has gone wrong. Make feedback a regular part of any performance development agenda. When employees are asked to come by your office for a special reason, you have already fostered anxiety and distrust of a necessary process. By building these conversations into routine events, employees know what to expect and will be more willing to see your point and work on changes.

Enough Already! Limit each session to one (at the most two) topics of performance to discuss. Don't bring a laundry list of wrong-doings. Even the most confident individual will feel bullied (no matter how good you may be at giving feedback).

"After You" Is More Than Just Good Manners. Allow the person receiving the feedback to have the opportunity to start the feedback. This is done by suggesting a self-assessment in the area(s) to be discussed. By starting out the session with the employee giving their own assessment of their performance or behavior in the targeted area, you avoid a crime-and-punishment type relationship. Take the employee's own self-evaluation and then see where your own notes are in sync.
Build on these points and then move into any points not discussed.

So What? If you cannot tie the behavior or issue to performance goals, you are probably being critical. For each piece of feedback you are about to give, make sure it can be tied to one of the employee's performance goals (or objectives, desires, agreements, or other predetermined criteria). Think through your real goal in giving feedback to ensure the best possible environment for receiving it.

Read on to master the art of feedback.

Feedback:
The Finer Points in Giving Feedback

I'll Have the "But Sandwich," Please. Balance the constructive with the positive. Avoid the "But Sandwich." Don't start out your session with a few nice things to say and then launch into the real reason for the feedback, then close down the session with a few more nice words. This is called the "but sandwich." It sounds something like this: You are doing a great job here, but… Any attempt at conveying positive feedback (and seeing a repeat of those behaviors) is lost using this method. It is necessary to show the employee where they can continue to make contributions, and where they can improve. Humans have both positive traits and areas for improvement. Acknowledge both.

Just the Facts, Ma'am. Do your research upfront. Include numbers, examples, and specifics. This isn't just a good idea to fend off defensive responses. It's vital to giving your employee full understanding of the situation, the impact, and your recommendation for improvement.

Likewise, if you want your positive feedback to really have some punch, and ensure a repeat performance, do the exact same thing.

Know Your Lines. Write out what you would potentially like to say before meeting with the employee. Better yet—practice with a trusted peer or loved one. Your use of words (and your body language) set the tone for a successful session. For instance, as mentioned previously in "Word Choice is Your Choice" avoid the words "never" and "always." No one is never or always any one way. You set up defensiveness with the employee and start a memory war of examples that contradict your statement.

Avoid the Horns or Halo Effect. This concept is generally found in interviewing. It refers to the tendency we all have to hire those that remind us of ourselves. The same phenomenon can be found when managing others. We tend to overlook mistakes made by those we identify with, and become hypercritical of those to whom we cannot relate. Before giving this person feedback (or withholding it), ask yourself if you are trying to make that person into a junior version of yourself, or is the behavior truly affecting productivity.

?

A Supervisor's Four Biggest Mistakes

In the 25+ years I have been working in human resources, I have been able to see firsthand the mistakes most often made by new and seasoned supervisors, managers, and others who lead employees.

Over time, I have consolidated these common errors into four major mistakes. See if you or someone in your organization is making these mistakes needlessly:

1. Giving feedback based on personality instead of based on data, behavior, or results. This phenomenon is seen when a management member tries to turn everyone on the team into a "mini-me." Certain that his or her style is the best, this supervisor offers advice, counseling, feedback, and even disciplinary action based on style or personality traits instead of on data, numbers, observed behaviors, and other objective criteria.

2. Failing to ensure someone's dignity at the beginning, during, and at the end of a one-on-one. The single most important component when giving someone corrective feedback is to ensure that person can walk away with dignity. When two people are in conflict or getting defensive (which is the main theme of most one-on-ones) this becomes increasingly difficult. In an attempt to appear in charge and in control, the supervisor may try to "win" by demeaning the employee with veiled insults, overheard gossip about the employee, or using statements like "everyone agrees with me."

3. Not accepting responsibility for every result produced by themselves and their team. Note that this mistake says every result. This is a very hard shift for many new management members. The new manager is no longer an individual contributor, and is now responsible for every person's performance. This is a contradiction in the "real world." We know that no one can control or change another. And yet, in management, you are expected to take responsibility for your team's performance, especially when it is lacking (and frankly, to not take credit when the performance is good!). The supervisor must determine what isn't working, and why, and correct that; and when things are working, he/she must continue these processes while ensuring everyone stays challenged, motivated, and recognized.

4. Not leading by example. Anyone who has had a moody boss knows that the tone of the day was set by this person's mood. To fail to show your "best face" regardless of the circumstances encourages similar behavior in your employees. This supervisor often doesn't see the correlation between his/her example and the team's mimicking behavior. Accusations of being unprofessional when employees arrive "just a little late," or when they begin to snap at co-workers, often come from this very supervisor. This inevitably leads to a lack of trust and performance that only follows the "just enough to not get fired" standard.

?

A Supervisors' Four Biggest Changes

How does a supervisor making the four biggest mistakes (see above entry) turn these around? By doing just that—turn around or reverse these mistakes and make them positives. Here's what this would look like:

1. **Focus on facts, not personalities**. Before talking with an employee, gather the data that supports your concerns. If your data doesn't support your pending constructive feedback, it's time to consider that you are judging this employee based on your own subjective criteria. This isn't just a bad management technique—it could also land you in court. In addition, when giving someone a "pat on the back," reinforce this recognition with the data that earned it.

2. **Ensure Dignity**. Ensuring another's dignity is possibly your biggest obligation as a management member. This may be why managers were invented. If someone feels they are being treated unfairly or have been wronged, it is the management member that is looked to as a corrective liaison. Another important factor in this step is to ensure your own dignity in every situation. To ensure another's dignity does not mean you sacrifice your own values or objectives. It also does not mean that you ignore your personal life or accept extra responsibility without a future payoff.

3. **Accept Responsibility for Results**. This is still the same advice as with the #3 mistake from the above entry. You have got to get your "arms around" this concept and deal with it. It is unfair and unreasonable, but it is the reality of management. Learning to work with others, especially those that are different from you (or that you don't like) is the first step. Learning conflict management techniques, listening skills, and all the other "soft" skills you have no doubt heard about, are the tools needed to accomplish this. Your parents and your school system did not teach you these skills, so it is up to you to learn them and USE them.

4. **Demonstrate Your Idea of Excellence**. This is a variation of "lead by example." The difference is that it is about demonstrating your idea of excellence. This means that instead of mimicking your boss or reading about leadership in a book, you decide what a leader does and says and stick to that. Aristotle said that excellence is a choice we make every day, and it is, therefore, not an outcome so much as a habit. Expect to make mistakes, but also look to remedy these errors. This is also demonstrating excellence (which is different from being perfect).

Friends at Work?

When I first started in my career, the rule of thumb was to keep work separate from your private life. Even then, I found myself making friends in the workplace. We often had to conceal our outside friendship for fear that someone would disapprove. Today, that seems almost laughable!

Compelling and long-standing research confirms that the #1 reason people stay with an organization is the social relationships (not to be confused with the #1 reason people leave an organization—lack of recognition or appreciation). While improving skills sets—and possibly salaries—are usually factors in choosing to leave an organization, the main reason people hesitate or turn down a new opportunity is concern about not fitting in with the new group.

Socially, we know we "mesh" with our co-workers in our current role. Will we also get along so well with others in a new organization?

Co-workers spend so much time together that our personal lives become a natural extension of this regular interaction. Baby showers, birthdays, divorces, illness are all acknowledged by our co-workers. These milestones are part of what we look back on when we reflect on our lives. As our co-workers are a part of these important moments, we can't help but forge long-term, and possibly lifelong, relationships.

If you are in management, consider this information. Instead of discouraging casual banter before a meeting, recognize it for what it is: relationship development. The more people enjoy each other's company and care about each other, the more productive the group, and the lower the turnover.

Where to start? Buy everyone lunch—for absolutely no reason. Allow for a quick birthday party in your office—someone brings a homemade goody and everyone born that month is honored. Quick, free, and effective in boosting the quality of your employees' morale.
⁇

The GOTCHA! Style

Are you a "Gotcha!" type of supervisor or person? The "Gotcha!" personality is that type of person who says nothing (or almost nothing) when things are going well—even perfectly—but swoop in like a seagull and POW! GOTCHA! when something isn't right. As managers, this type doesn't offer much in the way of recognition for a job well done. In fact, they often feel that a job well done is the status quo. Why waste time being a softy and acknowledging it?

While being good problem-solvers, Gotcha! types get stuck in this mode and spend most of their time scanning the horizon for what's not working, point it out, and then retreat. As spouses, parents, or co-workers, this type of style does a significant amount of damage. Since almost all interaction with a Gotcha! type is based on negativity, judgment, and correction, people in a Gotcha! person's life are likely to protect themselves. This might look like:

1. Lying
2. Getting defensive
3. Avoidance
4. Doing just enough to not get yelled at
5. Reciprocating with Gotcha! behaviors

Instead, the idea is to point out what is going well. Point it out often. The more we focus on what's working, the more we'll see these behaviors repeated. Then if correction is needed in the future, we can point out the positives, add the correction, and move on quickly. Important relationships will flourish and past resentments will start to die.

Say Cheese!

When writing reviews or having one-on-one discussions with employees or co-workers (or even family members), it can be helpful to have some key phrases to ensure the focus is on work-related performance. Using general statements over and over, or labels like "team player" or "attitude" are not useful. Instead, the idea is to specify what behaviors you would like to see repeated and which you would like to end.

For example, if someone has an "attitude," ask yourself, "What behaviors did this person exhibit before I decided he had an attitude?" These will likely be:

• Rolling eyes
• Not interacting with others
• Making negative comments during meetings
• Coming in late

What we often say instead is:

• Disrespectful
• Rude
• Not a team player
• Standoffish

The above words are just labels again. They are more specific ways of saying "attitude." You must focus on behaviors to give accurate feedback on performance. The rule of thumb is: If you can't capture the behavior on videotape, it can't be used in a review or coaching or feedback session.

In other words: body language, tone of voice, and word choice. These are the only three areas that would appear in your review or be spoken aloud.

Sentence Starters for Performance Feedback

Giving feedback is tough and not a habit for most of us. Try having some phrases prepared before you start that honor the suggestions provided in this section. Some good ones may be:

"When you (insert observed body language) during the discussion about the attendance policy, it indicated to me that you weren't in agreement. I'd like to talk about that now."

"Four out of the last five days you have been late (vs. 'you are never on time' or 'you're not punctual'). The attendance policy states…"

"About 40 % of what we communicate is through tone of voice. I overheard part of your conversation with that citizen and the tone of voice concerned me. I'd like to talk about that now…."

"Over the last six-month review period, your attendance has been 98%. This is well within our guidelines and your focus on punctuality has a positive impact on our ability to be responsive to customers."

"Over the last review period, your productivity in this area has decreased. Specific examples are… To improve this area, I would suggest…"

"Your performance this year has been exemplary. In order to keep you challenged, I would like to suggest several goals for the next review period…"

⍰

Why People Leave Jobs

The #1 reason we leave our jobs is not feeling appreciated. Most people assume it's about compensation, i.e., more money keeps people from leaving. Low salary is actually the #3 reason people move on. With something as inexpensive (and in many cases free) as appreciating someone, we can remedy excessive workplace turnover with just a few words.

People rarely leave jobs; they leave bosses and co-workers. Specifically, when an employee does not feel they are able to contribute in such a way that the organization benefits (the #2 reason for leaving: not able to make a meaningful contribution), an employee will look for an environment that allows for contribution and meaning.

It may seem on the surface that an employee's boss or HR department is responsible for giving recognition for a job well-done ('recognition' is fancy talk for appreciation!). But actually it's in all of our hands. Peers can provide appreciation as much as a supervisor. If one's supervisor is not the type to think about recognizing an employee's contribution, a peer can pick up that slack and allow for continued, productive employment. With 65 % of American workers going unrecognized last year alone*, the remedy lies in several options, not just formal recognition.

If this is true, why do people often leave an organization and say, "I am leaving for a better opportunity?" Once in a blue moon, a person gets a "tap on the shoulder" from an organization through their personal network. But the question I ask myself is: "Why were you looking for a better opportunity in the first place?"

If appreciation is lacking, productivity is lowered and turnover is increased. These results can cost an organization a significant amount of money in the short run and a damaged reputation in the long run.

Give Credit Where Credit is Due

Why not? As said before, recognition and appreciation are inexpensive and even free. With lack of recognition being the #1 reason people leave an organization, regular acknowledgement of a job well-done is time well-spent. It doesn't have to be difficult or expensive. For example, write an e-mail to a co-worker for something recently handled well. Even if it's their job, jot them a note thanking them for a consistent end result. Oh, and copy their boss while you're at it.

Many people in my workshops say to me, "Why should I give recognition when it's a person's job? They are getting paid, after all." This is usually said with a harsh tone as well. It seems to anger some people to have to recognize work that is expected.

Catching someone doing something right instead of only communicating when something goes wrong, is a strong motivator to continue doing good work. Likewise, if someone must go above and beyond the call of duty to earn another's praise, the likelihood of appreciation or recognition taking place regularly is going to be pretty low.

Why Recognition Isn't Optional

One research study indicated that when an employee is behaving negatively, they alienated every single customer they dealt with that day. Negativity often stems from a lack of appreciation. If that sounds like "fuzzy wuzzy" talk, just try acknowledging someone's contribution and test the theory.

If you don't observe an increase in energy and productivity, let me know (Stephanie@Work-Stress-Solutions.Com).

Okay, it is reasonable to feel at this point that a systematic appreciation process will result in a lack of impact. If you are considering creating an "Employee of the Month" award and rotate it each month, you are right. This insincere effort will generate embarrassment for the receiver and negativity among his coworkers.

On the other hand, providing appreciation in front of others increases the motivation levels tenfold. Recognize contributions in meetings or via e-mails (with key 'others' copied) for maximum impact. A public recognition of a job well-done gives that employee motivation for about *one month*. A salary increase is said to provide about *six weeks* of motivation (then it just becomes a regular paycheck again). You can usually give a salary increase about once a year; but recognition can be free or inexpensive and bears similar results and can be given all year long.

Lastly, make sure you are specific about what you appreciate. To say, "Good job" means nothing to another person and it is time wasted for you. Why? Because the person has no idea what to repeat or what to do again. Instead, offer behaviors and results. This sounds like, "*I was really grateful that you made it in during the snow day and answered the phones. It made the department look professional and saved us all a lot of catch-up work.*"

Do you think that individual will come in again during the next snow day? You better believe it.

Final Note: Trust Yourself

What if you started trusting yourself from this point on? What if you had all the knowledge you needed from books, seminars, and mentors and started trusting your own abilities, intuition, and ideas? Make this the last thing you read for a while. Start. That's all. Just start.

Suggested Reading and Other Resources

To read more about a certain topic or improve your workplace communications via the internet, I recommend the following:

Books
People Skills, Dr. Robert Bolton
The Seven Habits of Highly Effective People, Dr. Stephen Covey
Feel the Fear and Do It Anyway, Susan Jeffers
First Break All the Rules, Buckingham
Life Strategies, Dr. Phil McGraw
Silent Messages, Dr. Albert Mehrabian
The Worry Cure, Robert L. Leahy
The Disease to Please, Dr. Harriety Braiker
Leadership and Self-Deception, Arbinger Institute

Websites
Ezine Articles (ezinearticles.com)

VisionPoint Training Materials: Featuring reasonably priced training programs that are "ready-made" with leaders' guides that are easy to follow (no certification needed). Ken Blanchard is one of the founders (One Minute Manager author) and he brings the same uncluttered format to these programs.

CRM Learning: Explores workplace issues facing new supervisors and managers, offering guidance on these key issues to help define your management style: ethics, hiring, firing, and teamwork.

Workshops
Achieve Global/Zenger Miller Programs
American Management Association
DDI (Dynamic Dimensions International)
FranklinCovey and Myers-Briggs Type Indicator (rights owned by CPP)

About the Author

Stephanie Goddard is considered a subject matter expert in workplace communications and specializes in leadership, emotional intelligence and interpersonal skills training. Her experience includes both private and government sector clients.

Frequently appearing as a guest on radio programs and published in numerous articles on workplace communications, Stephanie is the author of *'101 Ways to Have a Great Day at Work'* which is an Amazon 'business-bestseller'; a SHRM bestseller; and has been translated into 15 languages.

She is also a nationally-certified trainer in:

-The Seven Habits of Highly Effective People®
-FranklinCovey's Project Management®
-The Skilled Facilitator®
-Covey's "First Things First" Time Management®
-FIRO® Element B® ABLE® Communication Preference Wheel®
-Dynamic Dimensions International (DDI) modules
-Master certification in Achieve Global's® leadership programs
-Ridge's "People Skills"®
-Myers-Briggs Type Indicator: MBTI®
-Crucial Conversations® Licensed Facilitator
-Goleman's Emotional Intelligence at Work™

Stephanie lives in Raleigh, NC where she creates and conducts workshops (and recently won the NaCo Award for "Best Training Program of the Year"). She provides training and one-on-one coaching to her local government's employees including EMS personnel, social workers, law enforcement officers, rescue workers, engineers, judges, librarians and city planners. She is also an instructor with the American Management Association.

For the latest resources in creating emotionally-healthy workplaces, visit Stephanie's website, **Work-Stress-Solutions.Com**. Contact Stephanie via email: Stephanie@Work-Stress-Solutions.Com

Manufactured by Amazon.ca
Acheson, AB

15545147R00088